Abbreviations

beg	begin, beginning
BO	bind off
cm	centimeter(s)
cn	cable needle
CO	cast on
dec	decrease
dpn(s)	double-pointed needle(s)
g	gram(s)
in	inch(es)
inc	increase(s)(ing)
k	knit
k2tog	knit two stitches together
k3tog	knit three stitches together
k4tog	knit four stitches together
kf/b	knit into front and then back of same stitch
kw	knitwise, as if to knit
m	meter(s)
meas	measures
ndl(s)	needle(s)
p	purl
p2tog	purl two together
pw	purlwise, as if to purl
rep	repeat
rnd(s)	round(s)
sl	slip
St st	Stockinette stitch
st(s)	stitch(es)
tbl	through the back loop
wyib	with yarn in back
wyif	with yarn in front
yd(s)	yard(s)
yo	yarnover

More and more, scarves and shawls are becoming must-have accessories—whether on the fashion show runway or in your own closet, scarves are a necessary part of any wardrobe. Every outfit should have a matching scarf or shawl to make it work.

In these pages you'll find scarves and shawls to suit every style: ten miles long, short and sassy, thick and fluffy, or light as a feather. Shawls can be made with simple stitches, bulky cables, or airy lace. Scarves can be as simple as a rectangle or as trendy as an infinity loop. There's something for every mood. Even if you don't need a scarf for winter warmth, you can wear a light cowl as a cover-up over evening wear, or a shawl to warm your shoulders on a cool autumn afternoon.

We know you'll be delighted by the beautiful scarves and shawls in this book—there's something to fit everyone!

Upstairs, Downstairs [NADJA BRANDT]

LEVEL OF DIFFICULTY
Intermediate

SIZE
67 x 10 in (170 x 25.5 cm)

MATERIALS
Yarn: CYCA #5 (chunky/craft/rug), Schachenmayr original Aventica or equivalent (25% Wool, 65% Acrylic, 10% Polyamide; 131 yd/120 m / 50 g), in Passion Color (#81), 300 g

Needles: U.S. size 9 / 5.5 mm circular ndl, approx. 32 in (80 cm) long

Notions:
9 st markers (optional)
Big-eye blunt tapestry needle

GAUGE
16 sts and 24 rows in St st = 4 x 4 in / 10 x 10 cm

Adjust needle size to obtain correct gauge if necessary.

This scarf can be worked so it is wider or narrower than the sample shown. Cast on a multiple of 7 stitches and work more or less than 7 repeats of the pattern for the desired width.

PATTERN STITCH
Following the chart, work the stitches to the right of the repeat once, then work the 7-stitch repeat 7 times across, then work the stitches to the left of the repeat once. Work Rows 1-8 once, then repeat Rows 9-22 for pattern. Only RS rows are charted. On WS rows, work the stitches as they appear.

INSTRUCTIONS
Using the stretchy cast-on, CO 63 sts, placing a marker after the first 8 sts, after each 7-st rep, and before the last 5 sts.

Row 1: Knit.

Work Rows 1-8 of chart once, then rep Rows 9-22 for pattern. After Rows 8 and 22, remove the last marker and place it after the beginning sts of the new rep on Row 9.

Work in pattern as set until piece measures 79 in (200 cm) long, or to desired length.

BO on WS.

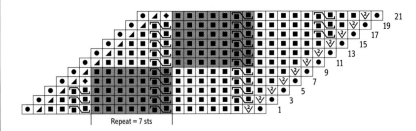

Repeat = 7 sts

● = Selvage: at beg of row, knit; at end of row, sl1 wyif

■ = K on RS and WS

◢ = k2tog on RS, knit this st on WS

Ⅴ = Kf/b

◥◣ = On RS, with cn, knit the 2nd st tbl, then knit the 1st st. On WS, purl the 2nd st then the 1st st

◆ = k1tbl on RS, k on WS

Twice as Nice [URSULA & MELANIE MARXER]

LEVEL OF DIFFICULTY
Experienced

SIZE
71 x 10½ in (180 x 27 cm)

MATERIALS
Yarn: CYCA #4 (worsted/afghan/aran), Lana Grossa Cool Wool Merino Big Superfine or equivalent (100% Merino; 131 yd/120 m / 50 g), Sand (#685), 350 g

Needles:
U.S. size 8 / 5 mm circular ndl
Cable needle approx. U.S. size 6 / 4 mm

Notions:
Tapestry needle

GAUGE
22 sts and 28 rows in Ribbing = 4 x 4 in / 10 x 10 cm

Adjust needle size to obtain correct gauge if necessary.

REVERSIBLE PATTERN
(Worked over a multiple of 9 sts + 3)

Row 1 (RS): P3, *k3, p2, p2 tbl, p2; rep from * to end.

Rows 2, 4 and 6: *K6, p3; rep from * to last 3 sts, k3.

Rows 3 and 5: P3, *k3, p6; rep from * to end.

Row 7: P3, *[yo, k3, turn; sl 1 pw, p2, wrap last worked st (bring yarn to front, sl first st from right needle to left needle, bring yarn to back, sl first st from left needle back to right needle), turn] 3 times; k3, turn; using cn, sl 1 pw, [p1, psso] 3 times, p2, turn—3 sts on cn; hold cn to front of work, transfer 3 sts from left needle to right needle; k3 from cn, then p3 from left needle; rep from * to end.

Row 8 (WS): K3, *p3, k2, k2 tbl, k2; rep from * to end.

Rows 9, 11, and 13: *P6, k3; rep from * to last 3 sts, p3.

Rows 10 and 12: K3, *p3, k6; rep from * to end.

Row 14: K3, *[yo, p3, turn; sl 1 kw, k2, wrap last worked st (bring yarn to front, sl first st from right needle to left needle, bring yarn to back sl first st from left needle back to right needle), turn] 3 times; p3, turn; using cn, sl 1 kw, [k1, psso] 3 times, k2, turn—3 sts on cn; hold cn to back of work, transfer 3 sts from left needle to right needle; p3 from cn, then k3 from left needle; rep from * to end.

Rep Rows 1-14 for pattern.

WRAP AND TURN
Wrapping a knit stitch: Sl1 pw wyib, move the yarn from back to front between the needles, move the slipped st back to the left ndl, bring the yarn to the back of the work between the needles.

Wrapping a purl stitch: Sl1 pw wyif, move the yarn from front to back between the needles, move the slipped st back to the left ndl, bring the yarn to the front of the work between the needles.

RIBBING
P3, k1, *p6, k3; rep from * 4 more times, p6.

SELVAGE STITCH
On RS, k2 for selvage; on WS, slip these sts pw.

INSTRUCTIONS
Using the Open Double Strand Cast On, CO 57 sts + 4 selvage sts—61 sts. Work 2-st selvage for the duration of the scarf, with pattern on the 57 sts in the center.

Work Rows 1-14 of Reversible Pattern 6 times, then work in Ribbing for 47 in (119 cm).
Work Rows 7-14 of Reversible Pattern once, then work Rows 1-14 five times, then work Rows 1-6 once more (84 rows worked).

BO all sts in Reversible Pattern. Weave in ends.

Braids and Buttons [VERENA HOFMANN]

LEVEL OF DIFFICULTY
Intermediate

SIZE
8¼ x 45¼ in (21 x 115 cm)

MATERIALS
Yarn: CYCA #4 (worsted/afghan/aran), Schachenmayr original Universa or equivalent (55% Merino, 45% Acrylic; 136 yd/124 m / 50 g), Red Wine Heather (#131), 150 g

Needles: U.S. size 8 / 5 mm circular needle, 47 in (120 cm) long

Notions:
4 buttons
Tapestry needle

GAUGE
29 sts and 34 rows in Cable pattern = 5 x 5 in / 12.5 x 12.5 cm

Adjust needle size to obtain correct gauge if necessary.

CHART
Page 90

GARTER STITCH
Knit every row.

CABLE PATTERN
Work in rows following chart. Work marked repeat 9 times across between edges. Only RS rows are charted. On WS rows, knit the first and last 7 sts for the front bands, and knit the bobble stitch; work all other sts as they appear.

INSTRUCTIONS
CO 253 sts and work charted pattern as foll: For the beg edge, knit 8 rows. Work Rows 9-57 with garter-stitch bands and cable center as charted, and on Rows 9, 25, 41, and 57, work buttonholes as charted. For ending edge, knit 8 rows. BO all sts.

FINISHING
Weave in ends. Sew buttons onto button band matching position of buttonholes. Fold scarf in half when worn so WS does not show.

Artful Brioche [UTE DORNHOF]

SIZE
Circumference: 44 in (112 cm)

Width: 16½ in (42 cm)

MATERIALS
Yarn: CYCA #3 (DK/light worsted), Schachenmayr original Extra Merino or equivalent (100% Virgin Wool; 140 yd/138 m / 50 g), Rubin (31), 200g

Needles: U.S. size 11 / 8 mm

Notions: Tapestry needle

GAUGE
13 sts and 18 rows in St st with 2 strands of yarn held tog = 4 x 4 in / 10 x 10 cm

Adjust needle size to obtain correct gauge if necessary.

BRIOCHE STITCH
Worked over an even number of sts.

Row 1: Selvage, k1, *yo, p1, rep from * to last 2 sts, k1, selvage.

Row 2: Selvage, k1, *yo, p2tog (working next yo and st tog); rep from * to last 2 sts, k1, selvage. Rep Row 2 for pattern.

This scarf is worked with 2 strands of yarn held together.

INSTRUCTIONS
With 2 strands of yarn held tog, CO 20 sts. Work in Brioche Stitch until approx. 1 yd (100 cm) of yarn rem and scarf measures approx. 44 in (112 cm). BO all sts, working each yo-st pair tog as 1 st—20 sts.

Sew the CO and BO edges tog to form a loop.

Weave in ends.

Allegretto [FRIEDERIKE PFUND]

SIZE
9 x 71 in (23 x 180 cm), without cord

MATERIALS
Yarn: CYCA #6 (bulky/roving), Schachenmayr select Alegretto or equivalent (30% Mohair, 40% Acrylic, 30% Polyamide; 34 yd/31 m / 50 g)

Yarn Amounts:

Ecru (8525), 250 g
Silver (8516), 150 g

Needles: U.S. size 17 or 12 mm circular needle and dpn

NOTE: There is no exact U.S. size match for 12 mm needles.

Notions: Tapestry needle

GAUGE
7½ sts and 14 rows in Seed Stitch = 4 x 4 in / 10 x 10 cm

Adjust needle size to obtain correct gauge if necessary.

SEED STITCH
Worked over an odd number of sts.
Row 1: Selvage, *k1, p1; rep from * to last 2 sts, k1, selvage.
Rep Row 1 for pattern.

INSTRUCTIONS
With Ecru, CO 3 sts. Work in Seed Stitch.
On Row 7, after selvage st, m1 (work inc into pattern).
Inc in this fashion every foll 6th row until you have 15 sts.
Work even in Seed St without inc until just before you finish the 4th ball of yarn. On the next row, then every following 6th row, after the selvage st (on the same side as the increases), k2tog.
When 3 sts rem, work another 5 rows in Seed Stitch. BO.

BORDER
With Silver, on the long edge of the scarf, pick up and knit 1 st for every 2 rows. Set this aside and cut yarn.

With dpns, CO 5 sts and make an I-cord (see page 96). Work 20 rows.
Slide the stitches onto the ndl with the scarf.
With dpn, k2, ssk (1 I-cord st and 1 st of sts picked up along edge of shawl). Slide the 3 sts just worked back onto the left ndl. *K2, ssk; slide sts back onto left ndl; rep from * until all picked up sts have been worked. **Next row:** kf/b twice, k1—5 sts. Work 20 rows of I-cord. BO.

Work the same edging on the other long edge of the scarf.

FINISHING
Weave in ends. Knot the two lengths of I-cord together at each end of the scarf.

Stand Out Beautifully [LYDIA KLÖS]

LEVEL OF DIFFICULTY
Experienced

SIZE
8½ x 51 in (22 x 130 cm)

MATERIALS
Yarn: CYCA #5 (chunky/craft/rug), Lana Grossa Alta Moda Cashmere or equivalent (80% Virgin Wool, 15% Cashmere, 5% Polyamide; 98 yd/90 m / 50 g)

Yarn Amounts:
Dark Gray Heather (10), 250 g
Petrol Heather (2), 100 g

Scrap yarn in contrasting color, small amount

Needles: U.S. size 10½ or 11 / 7 mm

NOTE: There is no exact U.S. size match for 7 mm needles.

Notions:
Cable needle
Tapestry needle

GAUGE
14 sts and 28 rows in Garter Stitch = 4 x 4 in / 10 x 10 cm

Adjust needle size to obtain correct gauge if necessary.

GARTER STITCH
Knit every row.

CABLE SLIP STITCH PATTERN
Work as charted. Only RS rows are shown. On WS rows, work all sts as they appear. Work the sts before the repeat once, then work the repeat across, then work the sts after the repeat once. Work each row in the color indicated on the chart, carrying the unused color up the side. Repeat Rows 1-12 for pattern.

SELVAGE STITCH
On RS and WS rows, knit this st, then give a tug on the yarn to tighten the st.

INSTRUCTIONS

COWL
With scrap yarn and provisional cast on, CO 38 sts and knit 1 row.
Join Light Gray Heather and begin working as charted, working the sts before the repeat once, then working the 6-st repeat sts twice, then ending with the sts after the repeat. Repeat Rows 1-12 until scarf is desired length, then work Rows 1-11 once more.
Remove the provisional cast on and place the live stitches on 3rd ndl; cut yarn, leaving approx. 60 in (150 cm) for binding off. Work across the row using 3-ndl BO, knitting the cable stitches and purling the rest.

HOOD
With RS facing, pick up and knit 66 sts across edge of scarf.
Work as charted, beg with Row 2 of chart (WS) and working selvage st at beg and end of every row. For pattern, work the sts before repeat, then work the 6-st repeat 7 times across, then work the sts after the repeat once. Work Rows 2-12 once, then repeat Rows 1-12 for pattern.

On Row 59, place marker after 33 sts.
On Row 60 then every other row 5 times, work in pattern to 2 sts before marker, k2tog, slip marker, ssk, work in pattern to end.
On Rows 64 and 70, to maintain pattern, work k2tog before and after the slip st to maintain pattern.
End after working Row 73.
Cut yarn, leaving a tail about 40 in (100 cm) long for binding off. Fold hood in half with RS tog.
Work across the row using 3-ndl BO, knitting the cable stitches and purling the rest.
Weave in ends.

Moody Loop [STEFANIE THOMAS]

LEVEL OF DIFFICULTY
Intermediate

SIZE
19½ x 16 in (50 x 40 cm)

MATERIALS
Yarn: CYCA #4 (worsted/afghan/aran), Lana Grossa Bingo or equivalent (100% Merino; 88 yd/80 m / 50 g)

Yarn Amounts:
Pink (117), 50 g
Natural (05), 50 g
Orchid (85), 50 g
Violet (128) 100 g

Needles: U.S. size 8 / 5 mm circular needle

Notions: Tapestry needle

GAUGE
17 sts and 23 rows in St st = 4 x 4 in / 10 x 10 cm

Adjust needle size to obtain correct gauge if necessary.

STOCKINETTE STITCH (ST ST)
Knit RS rows, purl WS rows.

BOBBLE
(Kf/b/f in the next st). Work 5 rows of St st back and forth on these 3 sts. On the 6th row (RS), sl1, k2tog, psso—1 st rem in bobble.

BOBBLE PATTERN
Rnd 1: *K1, p1; rep from * across.
Rnd 2: K1, p1, make bobble, *p1, k1, p1, make bobble; rep from * across, end with p1.
Rnd 3: Rep Rnd 1.
Rnd 4: *Make bobble, p1, k1, p1; rep from * across.
Rnd 5: Rep Rnd 1.

COLOR PATTERN
Work in St st in the round, following Charts 1, 2, and 3 and working 8-st repeat around. Work Rnds 1-28 of each chart once.

INSTRUCTIONS
With Violet, CO 80 sts and join to knit in the rnd, being careful not to twist sts. Work 5 rnds of Bobble Pattern. Work color patterns as charted, working 8-st repeat 10 times around. After all chart rnds are complete, work 5 rnds of Bobble Pattern with Violet.

BO all sts and weave in ends.

= K1 with Pink
= K1 with Violet
= K1 with Natural
= K1 with Orchid

Pattern 1

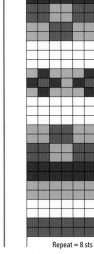

Repeat = 8 sts

Pattern 2

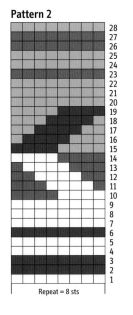

Repeat = 8 sts

Pattern 3

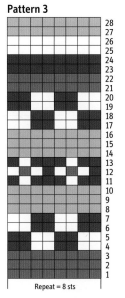

Repeat = 8 sts

Ribbed Stars [ANJA BELLE]

LEVEL OF DIFFICULTY
Intermediate

SIZE
6½ x 60 in (17 x 150 cm)

MATERIALS
Yarn: CYCA #4 (worsted/afghan/aran), Schoeller & Stahl Merino Mix or equivalent (51% Merino, 49% Acrylic; 109 yd/100 m / 50 g), Petrol (15), 150 g

Needles: U.S. size 7-8 / 4.5-5 mm, 24 in (60 cm) long

Notions: Tapestry needle

GAUGE
21 sts and 25 rows in Pattern Stitch = 4 x 4 in / 10 x 10 cm

Adjust needle size to obtain correct gauge if necessary.

STAR STITCH
P3tog, leaving original st on left ndl; yo, then p the 3 sts tog again.

PATTERN STITCH
Row 1: Knit all sts.
Row 2: *P1, make 1 Star Stitch; rep from * across, end with p1.
Row 3: Knit all sts.
Row 4: K3, *make 1 Star Stitch, p1; rep from * to last 2 sts, k2.

INSTRUCTIONS
CO 37 sts and, beginning with Row 2, work Pattern Stitch. Rep Rows 1-4 until scarf measures approx. 60 in (150 cm), or desired length, and end after working Row 2.
BO all sts. Weave in ends.
Wet scarf and dry flat to block.

Tip: This pattern is very loose and stretchy. The scarf will get much longer when blocked.

Colors on Fire [DAGMAR BERGK]

LEVEL OF DIFFICULTY
Experienced

SIZE
8 x 29½ in (20 x 75 cm)

MATERIALS
Yarn: CYCA #3 (DK/light worsted), Rowan Baby Merino Silk or equivalent (66% Superwash Wool, 34% Silk; 137 yd/134 m / 50 g)

Yarn Amounts:
Red (687), 100 g
Orange (686), 100 g

Needles: U.S. size 5 / 3.5 mm

Notions:
Scrap yarn
U.S. size G-6 / 4 mm crochet hook
Cable Needle
Tapestry needle

GAUGE
34 sts and 42 rows in Pattern Stitch = 4 x 4 in / 10 x 10 cm

Adjust needle size to obtain correct gauge if necessary.

PATTERN STITCH

Work RS and WS rows as charted. All rows of chart show sts as they appear on the RS of the work. The repeat is 34 sts. Work Rows 1 and 2 once, then repeat Rows 3-18 for pattern.

INSTRUCTIONS

With crochet hook and scrap yarn, ch 40. With knitting ndl and Red, pick up and knit 34 sts in the bumps on the back of the center 34 chains. Work as charted, ending after Row 17. Do not cut yarn.

Remove the crochet ch and put the live sts on ndl. Reversing RS and WS rows so braid lines up with Garter Stitch and vice versa, with Orange, work as charted, ending after Row 17. Do not cut yarn.

After Row 17, join Red and Orange sections as foll: Work the first 34 sts in Red, then work the next 34 sts in Orange, twisting yarn between colors to avoid a hole. The Red section ends with k2 and the Orange section begins with k2. Continue working over 68 sts in patterns as set, repeating Rows 3-18 for pattern, twisting yarns on the back of the work at the color change, until approx. 30 in (75 cm) of each color remains. BO all sts.

To wear the scarf, pull the ends through the loop formed by the hole between the two sections at the CO.

Tip: If you want to make a wider scarf, remember the opening should be about ¼ of the width of the scarf. A length of 30 in (75 cm) is about right for how this scarf is worn.

Blue Twilight [HEIKE ROLAND]

LEVEL OF DIFFICULTY
Intermediate

SIZE
10 x 65 in (26 x 165 cm)

MATERIALS
Yarn: CYCA #6 (bulky/roving), Lana Grossa Mille II or equivalent (50% Merino, 50% Acrylic; 60 yd/55 m / 50 g), Petrol (47), 500 g

Needles: U.S. size 11 / 8 mm

Notions:
Cable needle
Tapestry needle

GAUGE
24 sts and 15 rows in Cable Pattern = 4 x 4 in / 10 x 10 cm

Adjust needle size to obtain correct gauge if necessary.

CHART
Page 90

CABLE PATTERN
Work back and forth in rows as charted. Only Row 1 and RS rows are charted. On WS rows, work all sts as they appear. Work Rows 1-12 once then rep Rows 5-12 for pattern.

INSTRUCTIONS
CO 54 sts and work Cable Pattern as charted, with 1 selvage st at the beg and end of each row, until piece measures 65 in (165 cm). End after completing Row 5. On 6th row, BO in pattern. Weave in ends.

Soft Hues [HELGA SPITZ]

LEVEL OF DIFFICULTY
Intermediate

SIZE
8½ x 45 in (22 x 115 cm)

MATERIALS
Yarn: CYCA #0 (fingering), Lana Grossa Silkhair or equivalent (70% Mohair, 30% Silk; 229 yd/209 m / 25 g)

Yarn Amounts:
Blackberry (21), 50 g
Light Gray (35), 50 g

Needles: U.S. size 10 / 6 mm circular needle, approx. 32 in (80 cm) long

Notions: Tapestry needle

GAUGE
13 sts and 26 rows in Garter Stitch with 2 strands of yarn held tog = 4 x 4 in / 10 x 10 cm

Adjust needle size to obtain correct gauge if necessary.

GARTER STITCH
Rnd 1: Knit all sts.
Rnd 2: Purl all sts.
Rep Rnds 1 and 2 for pattern.

STRIPE PATTERN
Working with 2 strands of yarn held tog, work stripes as foll: *work 2 rnds in Blackberry, work 2 rnds in Light Gray; rep from * for stripes.

INSTRUCTIONS
With a double strand of Blackberry, CO 200 sts and join to work in the rnd, being careful not to twist sts. Work in stripe pattern for 8½ in (22 cm). BO loosely. Weave in ends.

Violet [DOROTHEA NEUMANN]

LEVEL OF DIFFICULTY
Experienced

SIZE
Circumference at bottom:
approx. 43 in (110 cm)
Circumference at top: approx. 25 in (65 cm)
Length: 19½ in (50 cm)

MATERIALS
Yarn: CYCA #4 (worsted/afghan/aran),
Schachenmayr original Soft Tweed or
equivalent (50% Wool, 50% Polyamide;
126 yd/115 m / 50 g), Violet, 200 g

Needles: U.S. size 7-8 / 4.5-5 mm, 24 in
(60 cm) long

Notions: Tapestry needle

GAUGE
15 sts and 26 rows in Pattern Stitch =
4 x 4 in / 10 x 10 cm

Adjust needle size to obtain correct gauge
if necessary.

CHART
Page 92

RIBBING
(K2, p2) around.

PATTERN STITCH
Worked over a multiple of 8 sts.
Rnd 1: *K4, p4; rep from * around.
Rnd 2: Knit all sts.
Rnds 3-9: Rep Rnds 1 and 2 three more times,
then work Rnd 1 once more.
Rep Rnds 1-9 for pattern.

SHAPING
Work 10 rnds in Pattern Stitch, then begin working 5-st rep around all sts as charted. Continue
following chart, with decs as shown, until all 89
rnds are complete.

INSTRUCTIONS
Using Twisted-Stitch Cast On and two strands of
yarn held together, CO 160 sts and join to work in
the round, being careful not to twist sts.

Work 6 rnds in Ribbing. On Rnd 7, work eyelet
rnd as shown on chart. Work main Pattern Stitch
(20 repeats in half of the round).
Work charted decreases every 10th rnd on each
5th rib repeat (marked in center of chart) 4
times—96 sts rem after all dec rnds completed.
Work main Pattern Stitch as set until piece measures approx. 19½ to 20½ in (50 to 52 cm). BO all
sts in pattern.

FINISHING
Wet and shape as desired to block.

Tip: To add a longer collar which can be used
as a hood approx. 4 to 6 inches (10 to 15 cm)
long, you will need about 250g of yarn.

Delicate Rose Petals [CHRISTIANE KLINK]

LEVEL OF DIFFICULTY
Experienced

SIZE
23½ x 71 in (60 x 180 cm); folded in half, 35½ in (90 cm)

MATERIALS
Yarn: CYCA #4 (worsted/afghan/aran), Rowan Kidsilk Haze or equivalent (70% Mohair, 30% Silk; 229 yd/209 m / 25 g), Fudge (658), 150 g

Needles: U.S. sizes 6 / 4mm and 8 / 5 mm, 24-32 in (60-80 cm) long

Notions: Tapestry needle

GAUGE
64 sts in Rose Pattern = 30 cm wide and 50 rnds in Rose Pattern = 20 cm high (see Tip at end of pattern) with larger needles

Adjust needle size to obtain correct gauge if necessary.

RIBBING
(K1, p1) around.

ROSE PATTERN
Worked over a multiple of 32 sts.
Work all rnds as charted. Work Rnds 1 and 2 once, then rep Rnds 3-26 for pattern. The repeat is 32 sts.

INSTRUCTIONS
This circular cowl is worked over 146 rnds: 12 rnds of ribbing at top and bottom edge, 2 setup rnds for the lace pattern, and 120 rnds (5 repeats of Rnds 3-26 of chart) of Rose Pattern.
With smaller circular ndl, CO 384 sts and join to work in the rnd, being careful not to twist sts. Work 12 rnds of Ribbing.

Change to larger ndl and work Rnds 1 and 2 of charted pattern once, then work Rnds 3-26 5 times (120 rnds).
Change to smaller ndl and work 12 rnds of Ribbing.
BO.

Tip: Be sure make a swatch before starting this cowl to ensure that you like the texture and look of the lace pattern. The exact gauge is not critical for this project. If you think the stitches on your gauge swatch are too tight, switch to a larger needle. If you think your swatch looks too loose, switch to a smaller needle.

Color Blocks [DOROTHEA NEUMANN]

LEVEL OF DIFFICULTY
Experienced

SIZE
8 x 63 in (20 x 160 cm)

1 square = 4 x 4 in (10 x 10 cm)

MATERIALS
Yarn: CYCA #3 (DK/light worsted), Schachen-mayr original Extra Merino or equivalent (100% Virgin Wool; 140 yd/128 m / 50 g)

Yarn Amounts:
100 g each of:
Off White (02)
Medium Gray Heather (092)
Orange (34)
Lavender (47)

Needles: U.S. size 5-6 / 3.4-4 mm

Notions: Tapestry needle

GAUGE
20 sts and 40 rows in Garter Stitch (20 garter ridges) = 4 x 4 in / 10 x 10 cm

Adjust needle size to obtain correct gauge if necessary.

GARTER STITCH
Knit every row.

INSTRUCTIONS
Each large square (8 x 8 in / 20 x 20 cm) is made from 4 smaller squares that are knit together. Starting at the bottom of the schematic drawing, follow the arrows for the direction of knitting. After all 4 small squares are complete, sew the beginning and ending together.

Each small square is 20 sts and 40 rows (20 garter ridges).

Following the diagram for the sequence of colors to use, CO 20 sts, knit 40 rows, and BO. *For the next square, on the left edge of the square just finished, pick up and knit 20 sts (1 in each garter ridge), knit 39 rows (20 garter ridges), then BO. Rep from * 2 more times.

Work 8 large squares.

FINISHING
Sew the squares together following the diagram. Weave in ends.

Tip: You can make the squares any size you like; just remember that you always knit twice as many rows as you have stitches! If you make this scarf with only 7 large squares, you will need about 50 g per color and the scarf will be about 55 in (140 cm) long.

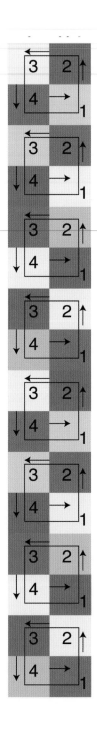

Tangerine [TANJA STEINBACH]

LEVEL OF DIFFICULTY
Intermediate

SIZE
14 x 51 in (35 x 130 cm)

MATERIALS
Yarn: CYCA #5 (chunky/craft/rug), Schachenmayr original Extra Merino Big or equivalent (100% Virgin Wool; 87 yd/80 m / 50 g), Orange (134), 250 g

Needles: U.S. size 9-10 / 5.5-6 mm circular needle

Notions: Blunt tapestry needle

GAUGE
16 sts and 24 rows in St st = 4 x 4 in / 10 x 10 cm

22 sts in Cable Pattern (unstretched) = 4 in / 10 cm wide

Adjust needle size to obtain correct gauge if necessary.

STOCKINETTE STITCH (ST ST)
Knit RS rows, purl WS rows.

REVERSE STOCKINETTE STITCH (REV ST ST)
Purl RS rows, knit WS rows.

CABLE PATTERN
Work over 22 sts as charted. Only RS rows are shown. Work all sts on WS rows as they appear. Rep Rows 1-6 for pattern.

HORIZONTAL RIBBING
Work 2 rows in St st, then 4 rows in Rev St st. Rep these 6 rows for pattern.

SELVAGE STITCH
Knit the first and last st of every row.

INSTRUCTIONS
Scarf is knitted sideways; then the ends are sewn together to form a loop.

CO 64 sts and purl 1 WS row.

Setup Row: Selvage st, pm; work 27 sts in Horizontal Ribbing, 22 sts in Cable Pattern, 13 sts in Horizontal Ribbing, selvage st—64 sts. Continue working patterns as set until piece measures approx. 51 in (130 cm), ending after Row 5 of cable pattern. BO in pattern.

FINISHING
Sew the CO and BO ends together, forming the scarf into a loop. Weave in ends.

Tip: For a more professional finish, you can use a provisional CO and join the ends with Kitchener stitch instead of sewing a seam.

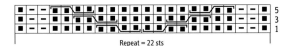

Repeat = 22 sts

■ = K1

— = P1

= Sl 2 sts to cn and hold in front, k2, k2 from cn

= Sl 2 sts to cn and hold in back, k2, k2 from cn

Shoulder Wrap [EVELYN HASE]

LEVEL OF DIFFICULTY
Intermediate

SIZE
41½ x 9 in (105 x 23.5 cm)

MATERIALS
Yarn: CYCA #4 (worsted/afghan/aran), Schachenmayr original Soft Tweed or equivalent (50% Wool, 50% Polyamide; 126 yd/115 m / 50 g), Violet (49), 150 g

Needles: U.S. size 6 / 4 mm
2 dpn approx. U.S. size 6 / 4 mm

Notions:
1 snap
3 silver beads
Tapestry needle

GAUGE
14 sts and 27 rows in St st = 4 x 4 in / 10 x 10 cm

Adjust needle size to obtain correct gauge if necessary.

GARTER STITCH
Knit every row.

STOCKINETTE STITCH (ST ST)
Knit RS rows, purl WS rows.

REVERSE STOCKINETTE STITCH (REV ST ST)
Purl RS rows, knit WS rows.

LADDER PATTERN
RS rows: Selvage, k1, *k1tbl, p1, k1tbl; rep from * across, end with k1, selvage.
WS rows: Work all sts as they appear, working knits tbl.

INSTRUCTIONS
CO 40 sts. Work 2 rows Rev St st, then 1 row St st, then begin working in Ladder pattern.

When piece measures 11 in (28 cm), work short-row shaping as foll:
Next row (RS): Work to last 2 sts, leave these 2 sts unworked, turn.
Next row (WS): Make a double stitch (see page 95), and work in pattern to end of row.
Rep last 2 rows, working 2 fewer sts in each RS row and working rem sts in Ladder pattern, until all sts have been used up.

Next row (RS): Knit across working each double-stitch as 1 knit.
Work 1 row in St st, then 2 rows in rev St st, then 1 row in St st.
Next row (RS): Work 3 sts in Ladder st, turn.
Next row (WS): Make a double stitch and work in pattern to end of row.
Next row: Work 5 sts in Ladder st, working double-stitch as 1 st, turn.
Rep last 2 rows, working 2 more sts in each RS row and working all sts in Ladder pattern, until all sts are back in work.
Work even in Ladder Pattern for 22 in (58 cm).
Work 1 row St st, then 2 rows in St st, then BO all sts pw.

FINISHING
Make an I-cord 24 in (60 cm) long as foll: Using a dpn, CO 4 sts. Do not turn, *slide sts to other end of dpn, draw yarn snugly across back of work, k4. Rep from * until cord is desired length. Fold the cord to form loops as the petals of a flower and stitch in place on the right upper corner of the shawl. Sew on snap buttons on the left upper corner of the shawl and sew the beads in the center of the flower.

Ruffles and Frills [URSULA & MELANIE MARXER]

LEVEL OF DIFFICULTY
Intermediate

SIZE
47¼ x 7¾ in (120 x 20 cm)

MATERIALS
Yarn: CYCA #4 (worsted/afghan/aran), Lana Grossa Evento or equivalent (65% Cotton, 35% Merino; 175 yd/160 m / 50 g), Lilac/Gray (41), 250 g

Needles:
U.S. size 7 / 4.5 mm circular needle
2 U.S. size 5 / 3.5 mm circular needles

Notions: Tapestry needle

GAUGE
20 sts and 28 rows in St st with larger needle = 4 x 4 in / 10 x 10 cm

Adjust needle size to obtain correct gauge if necessary.

PATTERN STITCH
Work as charted. Only RS rows are shown. On WS rows, purl all sts and on Rows 23-32, work all sts as they appear. Work repeat of 26 sts across then work last 5 sts once. Repeat Rows 1-54 once for pattern.

RIBBING
Selvage stitch, *p1, k1; rep from * across, ending with selvage st.

TUNNEL
With smaller ndl, work in Ribbing. To create the tunnel, using 2 ndls, k1, m1 on front ndl, k1, m1 on back ndl across. On next rows (Rows 23-32 of chart), work ribbing separately on each ndl, creating a double layer of fabric.

INSTRUCTIONS
Scarf is knit sideways.

With larger ndl and 2 strands of yarn held together, using twisted cast on, CO 707 sts + 2 selvage sts—709 sts.

Work Rows 1-22 of chart—164 sts rem (162 pattern sts + 2 selvage sts).

Over the next 10 rows (Rows 23-32), work Tunnel in Ribbing—328 sts.

Next row: K2tog across (working 1 front stitch and 1 back stitch tog)—164 sts (162 pattern sts + 2 selvage sts).

Work Rows 33-54—709 sts (707 pattern sts + 2 selvage sts).

BO all sts.

■ = K1

𝍣 = Central double decrease: slip 2 sts together knitwise, k1, p2sso

☐ = No stitch

─ = P1

✚ = Make 1: Insert the left needle under the bar between stitches from front to back, knit this through the back

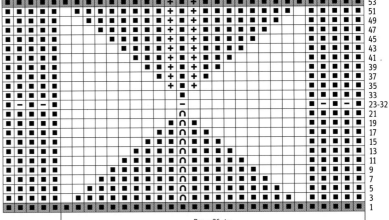

Rep = 26 sts

Cool Cables [ANDREA ADELHARDT]

DOUBLE SELVAGE STITCHES

On the prev row, slip the last 2 sts wyif. Turn. Knit into second st, leaving it on the left ndl, then knit first st and drop both sts from the left ndl.

RIBBING

K2, p2 across.

CABLE PATTERN

Work RS and WS rows as charted. All chart rows show what the fabric will look like on the RS of the work. Work the 8 st repeat across, then work the last 8 sts once. Rep Rows 1-8 for pattern.

INSTRUCTIONS

CO 37 sts and work as foll:

Row 1: Work double selvage sts and then work Cable Pattern starting on Row 3 of chart; end with 1 selvage st.

Row 2: Work all sts as they appear to last 2 sts, slip last 2 sts pw wyif.

Rows 3-6: Work Cable Pattern with selvages as worked above.

Rows 7-22: Work Rows 1-8 of Cable pattern 2 more times.

Rows 23-54: Work Rows 1-32 of Short Row chart once.

Rows 55-62: Work Rows 1-8 of Cable Pattern across all sts once.

Rows 63-94: Work Rows 1-32 of Short Row chart once.

Rows 95-102: Work Rows 1-8 of Cable Pattern across all sts once.

Rows 103-134: Work Rows 1-32 of Short Row chart once.

Rows 135-142: Work Rows 1-8 of Cable Pattern across all sts once.

Shawl center: Mark beginning and end of row with a piece of contrasting yarn.

Rows 143-150: Work Rows 1-8 of Cable Pattern across all sts once.

Rows 151-182: Work Rows 1-32 of Short Row chart once.

Rows 183-190: Work Rows 1-8 of Cable Pattern across all sts once.

Rows 191-222: Work Rows 1-32 of Short Row chart once.

Rows 223-230: Work Rows 1-8 of Cable Pattern across all sts once.

Rows 231-262: Work Rows 1-32 of Short Row chart once.

Rows 263-278: Work Rows 1-8 of Cable Pattern across all sts once.

BAND

Row 1 (RS): Work across row, working all sts as they appear; pm; pick up and knit 88 sts along side edge of scarf; pm; pick up and knit 37 sts along CO edge—162 sts. Markers indicate 38th stitch from each edge as increase points.

Row 2 (WS): Work double selvage sts, and, purling the marked corner sts when you come to them, *p2, k2; rep from * across, ending with p2.

Rows 3-14: Work in Ribbing as set, and m1 before and after the marked corner sts, working all incs into Ribbing pattern.

Work double BO as foll: Work next st in pattern, *work next st in pattern but leave original st on left ndl. Pass the 2nd st on the right ndl over the 1st (1 st bound off). Work the same st on the left needle again, this time tbl but leave original st on left ndl. Pass the 2nd st on the right ndl over the 1st, then drop the original st from the left ndl. Rep from * until all sts have been bound off.

LEVEL OF DIFFICULTY
Experienced

SIZE
Circumference: 14½ in (37 cm)

MATERIALS
Yarn: CYCA #4 (worsted/afghan/aran), Schoeller & Stahl Merino Mix or equivalent (51% Merino, 49% Acrylic; 109 yd/100 m / 50 g), Turquoise (36), 150 g

Needles: U.S. size 6 / 4 mm

Notions:
Cable needle
Tapestry needle

GAUGE
18 sts and 26 rows in St st = 4 x 4 in / 10 x 10 cm

Adjust needle size to obtain correct gauge if necessary.

CHART
Page 91

Grumpelino [NADJA BRANDT]

LEVEL OF DIFFICULTY
Intermediate

SIZE
63 x 11 in (160 x 28 cm)

MATERIALS
Yarn: CYCA #3 (DK/light worsted), Schachenmayr original Juvel or equivalent (100% Wool; 116 yd/106 m / 50 g), Olive (575), 300 g

Needles: U.S. size 7 / 4.5 mm circular needle, approx. 32 in (80 cm) long

Notions:
5 stitch markers
Blunt, large-eyed tapestry needle

GAUGE
22 sts and 24 rows in Pattern Stitch =
4 x 4 in / 10 x 10 cm

Adjust needle size to obtain correct gauge if necessary.

PATTERN STITCH
Worked over a multiple of 24 + 9 sts + 2 selvage sts.

Work as charted, working sts before rep once, then working 24-st rep across, then working sts after rep once. Only RS rows are charted. Work all sts on WS rows as they appear. Selvage st: At beg of row, k1-tbl, at end of row, sl1 wyif. Rep Rows 1-16 for pattern.

INSTRUCTIONS
With Stretchy Cast-On, CO 59 sts.

Row 1: Work all chart sts as foll: K1-tbl (selvage st), k3, pm; *k12, pm; rep from * 3 times. K6, sl1 wyif (selvage st).

Work in patterns as set until about 60-78 in (150-200 cm) of yarn is left or scarf is desired length. BO on WS.

Tip: Block this scarf flat for a wider scarf. Or, if you prefer a textured look, wash and dry flat without stretching and let the fabric retain its texture and wavy edges.

Rep = 24 sts

15
13
11
9
7
5
3
1

■ = K1
— = P1
● = Selvage st: At beg of row, k1-tbl, at end of row, sl1 wyif

Hello Sunshine [URSULA & MELANIE MARXER]

LEVEL OF DIFFICULTY
Intermediate

SIZE
71 x 10 in (180 x 25 cm)

MATERIALS
Yarn: CYCA #4 (worsted/afghan/aran), Lana Grossa Cool Wool Merino Big Superfine or equivalent (100% Merino; 131 yd/120 m / 50 g), Yellow (903), 500 g

Needles: U.S. size 6 / 4 mm circular needle

Notions: Tapestry needle

GAUGE
25 sts and 42 rows in Half Brioche Stitch = 4 x 4 in / 10 x 10 cm

Adjust needle size to obtain correct gauge if necessary.

HALF BRIOCHE STITCH
Row 1: *K1, p1; rep from * across.
Row 2: Knit all sts as they appear (knit the knits and purl the purls).
Row 3: *K1 in the row below, p1; rep from * across.
Row 4: Rep Row 2.
Work Rows 1 and 2 once, then rep Rows 3 and 4 for pattern.

BRIOCHE SELVAGE
On RS rows, k3.
On WS rows, slip 3 pw wyif.

INSTRUCTIONS
With 2 strands of yarn held tog and twisted cast-on, CO 63 sts.
*Row 1 (RS): Work 3-st Brioche Selvage, 55 sts in Half Brioche Stitch, k2tog, yo, 3-st Brioche Selvage.
Row 2 (and all WS rows): Work all sts as they appear, purling the yarn-overs.
Row 3: Work 3-st Brioche Selvage, 54 sts in Half Brioche Stitch, k2tog, 1 st in Half Brioche St, yo, 3-st Brioche Selvage.

Continue in this fashion with 1 less st of Half Brioche before the decrease and 1 more stitch of Half Brioche after the decrease on every RS row until no more Half Brioche remains before dec. Work the yarn overs into the Half Brioche pattern.
Work 1 WS row.

Next, work the diagonal line in the opposite direction as foll:

Row 1 (RS): Work 3 st Brioche Selvage, yo, ssk, 55 sts in Half Brioche, 3-st Brioche Selvage.
Row 2 (and all WS rows): Work all sts as they appear, purling the yarn-overs.
Row 3: Work 3-st Brioche Selvage, yo, 1 st in Half Brioche, ssk, 54 sts in Half Brioche, 3-st Brioche Selvage.
Continue in this fashion with 1 more st of Half Brioche before the decrease and 1 less stitch of Half Brioche after the decrease on every RS row until no more Half Brioche remains after dec. Work the yarn overs into the Half Brioche pattern.
Work 1 WS row.
Repeat the diagonal sections from * 3 more times, then BO all sts.
Weave in ends.

Diagonal Beauty [ANJA BELLE]

LEVEL OF DIFFICULTY
Easy

SIZE
4½ x 53 in (11.5 x 135 cm)

MATERIALS
Yarn: CYCA #1 (sock/fingering/baby), Schoppel Crazy Zauberball or equivalent (75% Wool, 25% Polyamide; 459 yd/420 m / 100 g), Autumn Sun (1537), 100g

CYCA #1 (sock/fingering/baby), Schoppel Admiral or equivalent (75% Wool, 25% Polyamide; 459 yd/420 m / 100 g), Steel Gray (9509), 100g

Needles: Approx. U.S. size 1-2 or 2.5-3 mm circular needle

NOTE: There is no exact U.S. size match for 2.5-3 mm needles.

Notions: Tapestry needle

GAUGE
21 sts and 48 rows in Pattern Stitch = 4 x 4 in / 10 x 10 cm

Adjust needle size to obtain correct gauge if necessary.

STOCKINETTE STITCH (ST ST)
Knit RS rows, purl WS rows.

REVERSE STOCKINETTE STITCH (REV ST ST)
Purl RS rows, knit WS rows.

PATTERN STITCH
Work 4 rows of St st in Autumn Sun and 4 rows of Rev St st in Steel Gray for stripes.

Carry the unused color up the side. On every first WS row, work the last st with both colors.

INSTRUCTIONS
With Autumn Sun, CO 4 sts and work in Pattern Stitch.

Increase Section: On every RS row, m1 after the first st and before the last st of the row until you have 60 sts.

Center Section: On every RS row, m1 after the first st and work the last 2 sts tog (k2tog or p2tog as needed to maintain pattern). Continue until scarf measures approx. 53 in (135 cm) along the right edge.

Decrease Section: On every RS row, work the first 2 sts tog and the last 2 sts tog (k2tog or p2tog as needed to maintain pattern). When 4 sts rem, BO.

Weave in ends.

Tip: Wash and dry flat to block. Be careful not to stretch the ribbing flat or it will lose its elasticity.

Ribbed in Brioche [URSULA & MELANIE MARXER]

HALF BRIOCHE STITCH

Row 1: *K1, p1; rep from * across.

Row 2: Knit all sts as they appear (knit the knits
and purl the purls).

Row 3: *K1 in the row below, p1; rep from *
across.

Row 4: Rep Row 2.

Work Rows 1 and 2 once, then rep Rows 3 and 4
for pattern.

SHORT ROWS

On RS rows, end 1 st before the end of the previ-
ous row and leave this st unworked on the left
ndl. Turn and work back on the following row.
Continue in this fashion working 1 less st in each
row until only the selvage st is worked. Then
work back across all sts in Half Brioche as set.

INSTRUCTIONS

CO 45 sts and work 54 rows (6 in / 15 cm) in Half
Brioche Stitch.

Continue in pattern as set and work shaping as
foll: *Work short rows, then work 12 rows in Half
Brioche Stitch over all sts; rep from * 9 more
times. Work short rows once more, then work 54
rows (6 in / 15 cm) in Half Brioche Stitch over all
sts.

BO. Weave in ends.

Casual Lace [STEPHANIE VAN DER LINDEN]

LEVEL OF DIFFICULTY
Experienced

SIZE
10 x 63 in (26 x 160 cm)

MATERIALS
Yarn: CYCA #4 (worsted/afghan/aran), Atelier Zitron Gobi or equivalent (40% Merino, 30% Camel, 30% Alpaca; 88 yd/80 m / 50 g), Gray-Blue (24), 250 g

Needles: U.S. size 9 / 5.5 mm circular needle, 24 in long

Notions: Tapestry needle

GAUGE
17 sts and 22 rows in St st = 4 x 4 in / 10 x 10 cm

17 sts and 26 rows in Lace pattern = 4 x 4 in / 10 x 10 cm

Adjust needle size to obtain correct gauge if necessary.

GARTER STITCH
Knit every row.

LACE PATTERN
Work as charted. On WS rows that are not charted, knit all sts including yarn-overs. On WS rows that are charted, stitches are charted as they appear on the RS of the work. Work WS Rows 4 and 12 as charted. Work the 16-st repeat across, then work the 1 st after the rep once. Rep Rows 1-16 for pattern.

INSTRUCTIONS
For beginning edge, CO 43 sts and work 8 rows in Garter Stitch.

Set up lace pattern as foll: K5, work Lace Pattern across to last 5 sts, k5.

Work in patterns as set with Garter Stitch at beg and end of rows and Lace Pattern in the center until 384 rows have been worked (24 repeats of Rows 1-16 of chart).

For ending edge, work 7 rows in Garter Stitch.

BO all sts knitwise.

Weave in ends carefully on the WS.

Wet shawl and block to dimensions.

Repeat = 16 sts

■ = K1
○ = Yarn over
◤ = Ssk (on WS rows, ssp)
◢ = K2tog
⋒ = Central double decrease: Sl2 tog kw, k1, p2sso
▲ = K3tog
□ = No stitch

Rustic Cables [UTE DORNHOF]

LEVEL OF DIFFICULTY
Intermediate

SIZE
90½ x 8 in (230 x 20 cm)

MATERIALS
Yarn: CYCA #4 (worsted/afghan/aran), Schachenmayr original Soft Tweed or equivalent (50% Wool, 50% Polyamide; 126 yd/115 m / 50 g), Sand (05), 250 g

Needles: U.S. size 7 / 4.5 mm
Cable needle approx. U.S. size 7 / 4.5 mm

Notions: Tapestry needle

GAUGE
16 sts and 22 rows in St st = 4 x 4 in / 10 x 10 cm

Adjust needle size to obtain correct gauge if necessary.

4-STITCH CABLE
Sl 2 sts to cn and hold in front of work, k2, then k2 from cn. On the following WS row, purl these 4 sts.

PATTERN STITCH
Worked over a multiple of 9 + 1 sts + 2 selvage sts.

Row 1: Work selvage st, *p1, k2, p4, k2; rep from * across, end p1, work selvage st.
Row 2: Work selvage st, *k1, p2, k4, p2; rep from * across, end k1, work selvage st.
Row 3: Rep Row 1.
Row 4: Rep Row 2.
Row 5: Rep Row 1.
Row 6: Work selvage st, *k1, p2, work 4-st cable over next 4 sts, p2; rep from * across, end k1, work selvage st.
Rep Rows 1-6 for pattern.

INSTRUCTIONS
CO 48 sts. Work in pattern stitch until scarf measures approx. 90½ in (230 cm). BO. Weave in ends.

Scent of a Rose [MANUELA SEITTER]

LEVEL OF DIFFICULTY
Experienced

SIZE
Inner circumference: 12 in (30 cm)

MATERIALS
Yarn: CYCA #6 (bulky/roving), Schachenmayr select Alegretto or equivalent (30% Mohair, 40% Acrylic, 30% Polyamide; 34 yd/31 m / 50 g)

Yarn Amounts:
Red (8501), 150 g
Orange (8523), 150 g

Needles: U.S. size 17 or 12 mm

NOTE: There is no exact U.S. size match for 12 mm needles.

Notions:
Elastic thread
Tapestry needle

GAUGE
1 rosette = 4 in (10 cm) in circumference
Adjust needle size to obtain correct gauge if necessary.

ROSETTE
CO 6 sts.

Row 1 (WS): Purl all sts.

Row 2: Kf/b in each st—12 sts.

Row 3: Purl all sts.

Row 4: (K1, kf/b in the next st) across—18 sts.

Row 5: Purl all sts.

Row 6: BO.

Roll the strip into a rosette shape and secure with a few sts in the center. Weave in ends.

INSTRUCTIONS
Make 13 rosettes in Orange and 13 in Red. Arrange 9 rosettes of Orange and Red in a circle with a diameter of 12 in (30 cm) and sew them together. Place the remaining rosettes on the bottom edge of the cowl and sew in place. Gather the neck edge in with elastic thread.

Wild Beauty [URSULA & MELANIE MARXER]

LEVEL OF DIFFICULTY
Experienced

SIZE
9½ x 63 in (24 x 160 cm)

MATERIALS
Yarn: CYCA #4 (worsted/afghan/aran), Lana Grossa Alta Moda Alpaca or equivalent (90% Alpaca, 5% Virgin Wool, 5% Polyamide; 153 yd/140 m / 50 g)

Yarn Amounts:
Taupe (15), 150 g
Dark Gray Heather (22), 150 g

Needles: U.S. size 10½ or 11 / 7 mm circular needle

NOTE: There is no exact U.S. size match for 7 mm needles.

Notions: Tapestry needle

GAUGE
14½ sts and 21 rows in Double Knitting = 4 x 4 in / 10 x 10 cm

Adjust needle size to obtain correct gauge if necessary.

LEOPARD-SKIN PATTERN
Work in St st and Double Knitting technique, following chart. Work the repeat of 33 sts once, knitting each st in the color shown and purling its paired stitch in the opposite color. On RS and WS rows, work 1 selvage st with both colors. Work 24 repeat rows 14 times.

DOUBLE KNITTING TECHNIQUE
Cast on the desired number of sts with both colors held together.

Setup Row: For the selvage stitch, k1-tbl with both colors. Knit 1 with Taupe with both yarns in back, then bring both yarns to the front between the ndls and purl the Dark Gray Heather stitch with Dark Gray Heather. Continue to work across the row in this manner. For the end selvage, k1-tbl with both colors held together.

Begin working as charted, working each Taupe square as a knit followed by a purl with Dark Gray Heather and working each Dark Gray square as a knit followed by a purl with Taupe, remembering to bring both yarns to the back of the work for knitting and to the front of the work for purling, so the unused yarns are stranded between the two layers of fabric.

All charted rows show the RS of the fabric, so remember to reverse colors on WS rows.

To BO, work all sts with both colors held together.

INSTRUCTIONS
CO 35 sts with Taupe and Dark Gray Heather held together—70 sts = 35 stitch pairs.
Work in Leopard-Skin Pattern for 63 in (160 cm).
BO with both colors held tog.

FINISHING
Weave in ends. Wet the scarf and dry flat to block.

■ = K1 in Taupe / P1 in Dark Gray Heather
■ = K1 in Dark Gray Heather / P1 in Taupe

Pattern = 33 sts

Waves [STEPHANIE VAN DER LINDEN]

LEVEL OF DIFFICULTY
Intermediate

SIZE
10 x 47 in (25 x 120 cm)

MATERIALS
Yarn: CYCA #4 (worsted/afghan/aran), Atelier Zitron Nimbus or equivalent (100% Merino; 109 yd/100 m / 50 g)

Yarn Amounts:
Steel Blue (408), 100 g
Dark Violet (432), 150 g

Needles: U.S. size 6 / 4 mm circular needle 47 in / 120 cm long

Notions: Blunt tapestry needle

GAUGE
19 sts and 24 rows in Wave Pattern =
4 x 4 in / 10 x 10 cm

Adjust needle size to obtain correct gauge if necessary.

GARTER STITCH
Knit every row.

WAVE PATTERN
Work back and forth in rows as charted. Only RS rows are shown. On WS rows, purl all sts. Work the 17 st repeat 13 times across and rep Rows 1-4 for pattern.

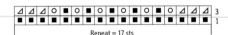

Repeat = 17 sts

◿ = k2tog
○ = yo
■ = k1

STRIPE PATTERN
* Work 4 rows in Steel Blue, then 4 rows in Violet; rep from * for stripe pattern. Carry the unused color up the side of the shawl and twist the yarns every other edge for a clean edge.

INSTRUCTIONS
With Violet, CO 223 sts loosely. Purl 2 rows. Begin following chart, knitting the first and last st of each row for a garter-stitch selvage, and changing colors every 4 rows for stripes.
After the 6th Steel Blue stripe, cut the blue yarn and work 4 rows in Violet.
Next row (RS): Knit.
BO all sts knitwise, loosely.
Weave in ends.

ROSE
With Violet, CO 66 sts and work 3 rows in Garter Stitch.
Next row (RS): *K6, rotate the left needle around the CO edge to twist the knitting; rep from * 10 more times.
Purl 1 row.
Next row (RS): K2tog across—33 sts rem.
Next row: K2tog across to last st, k1—17 sts rem.
Next row: K2tog across to last st, k1—9 sts rem.
Cut the yarn, leaving a tail about 12 in (30 cm) long, and draw the tail through the remaining sts. Curl the strip into a spiral and use the tail to tack the rose into shape and sew it onto the scarf.

Water Lily [CHRISTIANE KLINK]

LEVEL OF DIFFICULTY
Experienced

SIZE
24 x 59 in (60 x 150 cm)

MATERIALS
Yarn: CYCA #0 (fingering), Lana Grossa Lace Lux or equivalent (33% Virgin Wool, 67% Viscose; 339 yd/310 m / 50 g), Gray (16), 250 g

Needles: U.S. size 6 / 4 mm circular needle 24-32 in (60-80 cm) long

Notions: Tapestry needle

GAUGE
21 sts and 25 rows in Water Lily Lace pattern = 4 x 4 in / 10 x 10 cm

Adjust needle size to obtain correct gauge if necessary.

CHART
Page 93

WAVY EDGING
Worked over a repeat of 34 sts.
Work as charted, following sections marked A and D.
For the beginning edge, work Rows 4-17 of chart once.
For the ending edge, work Rows S5-S18 of chart once.

WATER LILY LACE PATTERN
Worked over a repeat of 16 sts.
Work as charted, following Sections B and C. On rows that are not charted, knit all sts and yarn overs.
Work Rows 1-28 (Section B) 4 times, then work Rows S1-S14 (Section C) once.

On even chart rnds that are not shown, knit all sts. Work even rnds that are included in the chart, such as R2, R20, RS2, RS20, and RS22, as charted.

INSTRUCTIONS
The cowl is worked in 169 rnds as foll: 22 rnds + 21 rnds for the Wavy Edging (Sections A and D) at the ends + 112 rnds in Water Lily Lace pattern (4 repeats of Section B) + 14 rnds to complete the lace pattern (1 repeat of Section C).

With circular ndl, CO 340 sts and join to work in the rnd, being careful not to twist sts. Work charts as follows.

BEGINNING BORDER
Beginning with Section A: Purl 3 rnds (Rows 1-3 of chart), then, for the Wavy Edging, work Rows 4-17 of chart.
On Rnd 18, dec 20 sts evenly spaced—320 sts rem.
Purl Rnds R19-R21, then knit Rnd R22.

CENTER
Work Section B of chart for Water Lily Lace Pattern, knitting on all uncharted rnds, including the yarn overs. Work Rows 1-28 of chart a total of 4 times. Finish the Water Lily Lace Pattern by working Section C, Rows S1-S14, once.

ENDING BORDER
Following Section D, purl Rnds RS1-RS3, then knit Rnd RS4; then, for the Wavy Edging, work Rnds RS5-RS17 as charted. End by knitting Rnd RS18 and purling RS19-21.
BO all sts.

FINISHING
Weave in ends. Wash, pin to dimensions, and dry flat to block.

Tip: Be sure make a swatch before starting this cowl to ensure that you like the texture and look of the lace pattern. The exact gauge is not critical for this project. If you think the stitches on your gauge swatch are too tight, switch to a larger needle. If you think your swatch looks too loose, switch to a smaller needle. For a longer cowl, repeat Rows 1-28 of the Water Lily Pattern one or two more times.

Wellness [HEIKE ROLAND]

LEVEL OF DIFFICULTY
Intermediate

SIZE
20½ x 43½ in (52 x 110 cm)

MATERIALS
Yarn: CYCA #6 (bulky/roving), Lana Grossa Olympia or equivalent (53% Wool, 47% Acrylic; 109 yd/100 m / 100 g), Blue-Purple (21), 300 g

Needles: U.S. size 11 / 8 mm circular needle

Notions: Tapestry needle

GAUGE
12 sts and 17 rows in Pattern Stitch = 4 x 4 in / 10 x 10 cm

Adjust needle size to obtain correct gauge if necessary.

PATTERN STITCH
Work all rnds as charted. Work the 16 st repeat 9 times around.

INSTRUCTIONS
With 2 ndls held together, CO 144 sts loosely. Join to work in the rnd being careful not to twist sts.

Work as charted, working Rnds 1-38 once, then work Rnd 38 another 34 times.

BO all sts. Weave in ends.

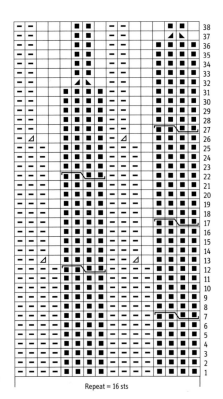

Repeat = 16 sts

■ = K1

— = P1

▐■▐■▐■▌ = Sl 2 to cn and hold in front, k2, k2 from cn

◢ = P2tog

◣ = On RS ssk, on WS ssp

◥ = On RS k2tog, on WS p2tog

☐ = No stitch

Lofty Elegance [LYDIA KLÖS]

GARTER STITCH

Knit every row.

EYELET PATTERN STITCH

Row 1 (RS): Knit.

Row 2 (WS): K4, *P4, yo; rep from * to last 4 sts, k4.

Row 3: K4, *yo, lift the yo from row 2 onto the right ndl, k2tog, k2, pass the lifted st over the 3 sts just worked; rep from * to last 3 sts, k4.

Row 4: K4, purl to last 4 sts, k4.

EYELET PATTERN WITH SHAPING

Row 1 (RS): Knit, ending before the last 6 sts; turn and place marker for turning point.

Row 2 (WS): Yo, p6, *p4, yo; rep from * across, ending before the last 6 sts; turn and place marker for turning point.

Rows 3 and 7: Yo, k2, *yo, lift the yo from row 2 onto the right ndl, k2tog, k2, pass the lifted st over the 3 sts just worked; rep from * across, ending 6 sts before marker; turn and place marker for new turning point.

Rows 4 and 8: Yo, purl all sts and yarn overs, ending 6 sts before marker; turn and place marker for new turning point.

Row 5: Yo, knit, ending 6 sts before marker; turn and place marker for new turning point.

Row 6: Yo, p6, *p4, yo; rep from * across, ending 6 sts before marker; turn and place marker for new turning point.

BORDER

Work as charted, beginning with Row 1. Only RS rows are charted. On WS rows, knit the dark gray sts and purl all other sts and yarn overs. Work the dark gray sts at the beginning of the row once, then work the repeat across, then work the dark gray sts at the end once. Rep Rows 1-26 once.

INSTRUCTIONS

CO 380 sts and work 5 rows in Garter Stitch. Begin working Eyelet Pattern Stitch. Work Rows 1-4 once, then begin working Eyelet Pattern with Shaping, working Rows 1-8 once then repeating Rows 5-8 another 13 times (64 rows in Eyelet Pattern).

Row 65: After turning, purl across and work each turning yarn over together with the following stitch as ssp; knit last 4 sts. Remove markers as you come to them.

BORDER

K4; work the 31 st rep across to last 4 sts, k4. On the first row, k2tog to work the last remaining turning yarnover with the following st. BO loosely.

FINISHING

Weave in ends. Wash, block to dimensions pinning out each point, and air dry.

■ = K on RS, P on WS
■ = Knit on RS and WS
○ = Yarn over
◣ = Sl1 kw, k1, psso
◢ = K2tog

▲ = Double dec: sl1 kw, k2tog, psso
▢ = BO with crochet hook
▲ = BO3tog with crochet hook
▨ = BO then draw yarn through to make 1 chain st

Repeat = 12 sts

LEVEL OF DIFFICULTY
Experienced

SIZE
12 x 71 in (30 x 180 cm)

MATERIALS
Yarn: CYCA #0 (fingering), Lana Grossa Lace Lux or equivalent (33% Virgin Wool, 67% Viscose; 339 yd/310 m / 50 g), Turquoise Heather (27), 100 g

Needles: U.S. size 5 / 3.5 mm

Notions:
2 removable stitch markers
Tapestry needle

GAUGE
20 sts and 34 rows in St st =
4 x 4 in / 10 x 10 cm

Adjust needle size to obtain correct gauge if necessary.

Watercolor Hues [STEFANIE THOMAS]

LEVEL OF DIFFICULTY
Easy

SIZE
6 x 57 in (15 x 170 cm)

MATERIALS
Yarn: CYCA #5 (chunky/craft/rug), Auster-mann Murano or equivalent (51% Wool, 49% Acrylic; 262 yd/240 m / 150 g), Purple (31), 150 g

Needles: U.S. size 11 / 8 mm circular needle

Notions: Tapestry needle

GAUGE
12 sts and 23 rows in Garter Stitch = 4 x 4 in / 10 x 10 cm

Adjust needle size to obtain correct gauge if necessary.

RIBBING
(K2, p2) across.

GARTER STITCH
Rnd 1: Knit all sts.
Rnd 2: Purl all sts.
Rep Rnds 1 and 2 for pattern.

INSTRUCTIONS
CO 200 sts and join to work in the rnd, being careful not to twist sts.

*Work 6 rnds in Ribbing, then work 7 rnds in Garter Stitch; rep from * once more, then work 6 rnds in Ribbing once more. BO all sts.

Weave in ends.

Fresh Flecks [TANJA STEINBACH]

LEVEL OF DIFFICULTY
Intermediate

SIZE
16 x 27½ in (40 x 70 cm)

MATERIALS
Yarn: CYCA #6 (bulky/roving), Schachenmayr original Lova or equivalent (30% Wool, 67% Acrylic, 3% Polyamide; 55 yd/50 m / 50 g), Beige-Orange Spots (87), 250 g

Needles:
U.S. size 13-15 / 9-10 mm circular needle, 24 in (60 cm) long
2 U.S. size 13 / 9 mm double-pointed needles

Notions: Blunt tapestry needle

GAUGE
11-12 sts and 16 rows in St st = 4 x 4 in / 10 x 10 cm

Adjust needle size to obtain correct gauge if necessary.

CHART
Page 93

SELVAGE
The selvage is worked over 3 sts.
On RS rows, work the first and last 3 sts as foll:
K2, sl1 wyif, k1.
On WS rows, work the first and last 3 sts as foll:
Sl1 wyif, k1, sl1 wyif.

RIBBING
Worked over a rep of 6 + 3 sts + 6 selvage sts.

The selvage sts are not included in the instructions below. See "Selvage" above.

RS rows: *P3, k1, sl1 pw wyib, k1; rep from * to last 3 sts, p3.
WS rows: Work all sts as they appear, purling the slipped sts.

SPIRAL PATTERN
Worked over a repeat of 6 sts.
Work all rnds as charted, working the 6 st rep continuously around. After the first round, pay careful attention, as the the ribbing will move in a spiral pattern.
Rep Rnds 1-24 for pattern.

INSTRUCTIONS
CO 81 sts and work in Ribbing for 8 in (20 cm), working the first and last 3 sts as Selvages. When piece measures 8 in (20 cm), k2tog 3 times at beg of row—78 sts.
Join in the round and work in Spiral Pattern over rem 78 sts for 8 in (20 cm).

ATTACHED I-CORD BO
CO 3 at beg of rnd. With dpn, *k2, ssk; slip the 3 sts from the dpn back onto the left ndl. Draw the working yarn snugly across the back to form a tube. Rep from * until all sts of scarf are bound off. BO rem 3 sts. Cut yarn and use tail to sew the beginning and end of the cord together. Weave in ends.

Patchwork in Pastels [DAGMAR BERGK]

GARTER STITCH
Knit every row.

PATCHWORK TECHNIQUE
Work following schematic for colors and direction of knitting. Do not BO sts at the end of each section. Leave live sts on the needle to be worked together with next section for seamless finishing. The diagram indicates the order in which to knit the sections as well as how many sts and rows to knit and which colors to use. The arrows indicate the direction of the knitting.

INSTRUCTIONS
The scarf is worked with 2 strands of yarn held together and Garter Stitch. The edge stitches are also knit on every row.

Section 1: With A and B held tog, CO 75 sts. Work 16 rows in Garter Stitch. Do not BO. Cut yarns.

Section 2: On the right edge (with the sts on the left ndl), with A and C held tog, CO 25 sts and work 50 rows. At the end of each RS row, ssk (last st of new section with next st of prev section joined). Cut yarns.

Section 3: With D and E held tog, continue working on same 25 sts work 17 rows and at the end of the 8 RS rows, ssk (last st of new section with next st of prev section joined). Cut E.

Section 4: With B and D held tog, work over the rem 42 sts of Section 1 and at the end of each WS row, ssk to join to live sts of section 3. Leave sts on ndl. Cut yarns.

Continue joining sections as you knit.

Section 5: On left edge with F and G, CO 18 sts and work 57 rows (first row is WS row), joining to Section 4 as you knit. Cut yarn and leave sts on ndl.

Section 6: On right edge with A and C, pick up and knit 25 sts over section 2, pick up and knit 8 sts over section 3, and work 14 sts over Section 4—47 sts total in Section 6, joining to Section 5 as you knit. Cut yarns.

Section 7: With E and H, work across 47 sts of section 6 and pick up and knit 28 sts over Section 5—76 sts. Work 16 rows. Cut yarn.

Section 8: Over the first 38 sts of Section 7, with D and G, knit 24 rows.

Section 9: Over the same 38 sts, with B and G, knit 8 rows. Leave the yarn attached and the sts on the ndl.

Section 10: On left edge of Sections 8 and 9, with C and H, pick up and knit 16 sts and knit 45 rows (ending with a RS row), joining to Section 7 with ssk. Leave the sts on the ndl. Cut C.

Section 11: On the rem 15 sts of Section 7, with 2 strands of H, knit 32 rows ending with a WS row and with the last st on the ndl, k2tog with first st of section 10. Cut yarns.

Section 12: With B and G (yarn attached to Section 9), work across the 38 sts of section 9, pick up and knit 22 sts across top of section 10, and work across the 15 sts of section 11—75 sts. Knit 8 rows.

Section 13: With C and F, knit 20 rows over all sts.

This completes the first of 3 blocks. Continue working on the same sts and work 2 more blocks (Sections 1-13) following the same schematic, but working colors as shown in table on page 93.

BO all sts. Weave in ends.

Tip: When a section starts with the same color as the last section ended, do not cut yarn. This reduces the number of ends to weave in later.

LEVEL OF DIFFICULTY
Experienced

SIZE
18 x 63 in (45 x 160 cm)

MATERIALS
Yarn: CYCA #0 (fingering),
Rowan Kidsilk Haze or equivalent (70% Mohair, 30% Silk;
229 yd/209 m / 25 g), 25 g
each of:
Ultra (659)
Mud (652)
Jelly (597)
Steel (664)
Blushes (583)
Alhambra (666)
Heavenly (592)
Dewberry (600)

Needles: U.S. size 5 / 3.5 mm

Notions: Tapestry needle

GAUGE
17 sts and 30 rows in Garter
Stitch = 4 x 4 in / 10 x 10 cm

Adjust needle size to obtain
correct gauge if necessary.

COLOR TABLE AND
SCHEMATIC
Page 92

Deep Blue Sea [HEIKE ROLAND]

LEVEL OF DIFFICULTY
Intermediate

SIZE
8 x 47 in (21 x 120 cm)

MATERIALS
Yarn: CYCA #5 (chunky/craft/rug), Austermann Murano or equivalent (51% Wool, 49% Acrylic; 262 yd/240 m / 150 g), Blue Nature (14), 150 g

Needles: U.S. size 11 / 8 mm

Notions: Tapestry needle

GAUGE
9 sts and 10 rows in Brioche Stitch = 4 x 4 in / 10 x 10 cm

Adjust needle size to obtain correct gauge if necessary.

BRIOCHE STITCH
Row 1: Selvage, *p1, k1; rep from * across, end with p1, selvage.

Row 2: Selvage, *k1, sl1 pw, yo; rep from * across, end with k1, selvage.

Row 3: Selvage, *sl1 pw, yo, k2tog (next st and the paired yo); rep from * across, end with sl1 pw, yo, selvage.

Row 4: Selvage, *k2tog (next st and the paired yo), sl1 pw, yo; rep from * across, end with k2tog, selvage.

Work Rows 1-4 once, then rep Rows 3 and 4 for pattern.

INSTRUCTIONS
CO 23 st and work in Brioche Stitch until yarn is almost used up. BO all sts. Sew the CO and BO ends together to form a loop. Weave in ends.

Puffy Triangles [DAGMAR BERGK]

LEVEL OF DIFFICULTY
Experienced

SIZE
Width: 10 in (25 cm)
Length at inner edge: 47 in (120 cm)
Length at outer edge: 71 in (180 cm)

MATERIALS
Yarn: CYCA #3 (DK/light worsted), Rowan Felted Tweed or equivalent (50% Merino, 25% Alpaca, 25% Viscose; 191 yd/175 m / 50 g), Peony (183), 150 g

Needles: U.S. size 5 / 3.5 mm

Notions: Tapestry needle

GAUGE
22 sts and 29 rows in Pattern Stitch = 4 x 4 in / 10 x 10 cm

Adjust needle size to obtain correct gauge if necessary.

SEED STITCH
Worked over an even number of sts.
Row 1: (K1, p1) across.
Row 2: (P1, k1) across.
Rep Rows 1 and 2 for pattern.

PATTERN STITCH
Worked over a multiple of 12 + 6 sts.
Row 1: Knit.
Row 2 (and all WS rows): Purl.
Row 3: *Yo, k4, k2tog, turn, p5, turn, yo, k4, k2tog, turn, p3, turn, yo, k2, k2tog, turn, p3, turn, yo, k1, k2tog, turn, p2, turn, yo, k2tog, turn (first triangle complete), k6 (distance to next triangle); rep from * 2 more times, then k6 once more.
Row 5: Knit.
Row 7: K6 then work as for Row 3, ending with triangle.
Row 8: Purl.
Rep Rows 1-8 for pattern.

INSTRUCTIONS
CO 54 sts. Work 8 rows in Seed Stitch.
Setup patterns as foll: Work 6 sts in Seed Stitch, 42 sts in Pattern Stitch (3 repeats of 12, plus 6 sts), 6 sts in Seed stitch.
Maintaining patterns as set, end after working 12 rows.
Work short rows as foll:
Row 13: Work 6 sts in Seed Stitch, 12 sts in Pattern Stitch, turn.
Row 14: Sl1 pw, purl to last 6 sts, work 6 sts in Seed Stitch.

Row 15: Work 6 sts in Seed Stitch, 30 sts in Pattern Stitch, and in the 19th st (turning st from Row 13) lift the right leg of the slipped stitch from the row below and knit it together with the next st to hide the hole at the turning point; turn.
Row 16: Sl1 pw, purl to last 6 sts, work 6 sts in Seed Stitch.
Row 17: Work in patterns as set, hiding turning hole as above.
Row 18: Purl.
Row 19: Rep Row 15.
Row 20: Rep Row 16.
Row 21: Rep Row 13.
Row 22: Rep Row 14.
Rep patterns as at the beginning (6 sts in Seed Stitch, 42 sts in Pattern Stitch, 6 sts in Seed Stitch), but offset the position of the triangles by starting with Rows 7-8, then working Rows 3-8. Work short row section (Rows 13-22) once again. Repeat plain and short row section 10 times, then end with Rows 3-8 so both ends match.
Next row (RS): Work 6 sts in Seed Stitch, k42, 6 sts in Seed Stitch.
Next row (WS): Work 6 sts in Seed Stitch, p42, 6 sts in Seed Stitch.
Work 8 rows in Seed Stitch. BO all sts.

Houndstooth & Co. [WALTRAUD RÖHNER]

LEVEL OF DIFFICULTY
Intermediate

SIZE
7 x 51 in (18 x 130 cm)

MATERIALS
Yarn: CYCA #1 (sock/fingering/baby), Schoppel Zauberball or equivalent (75% Wool, 25% Polyamide; 459 yd/420 m / 100 g), Shadow (1508), 20 g

CYCA #1 (sock/fingering/baby), Schoppel Admiral or equivalent (75% Wool, 25% Polyamide; 459 yd/420 m / 100 g), Olive (383), 200 g

Needles: 2 U.S. size 1½ / 2.5 mm circular needles, 24 in (60 cm) long

Notions:
Stitch marker
Tapestry needle

GAUGE
34 sts and 43 rows in St st = 4 x 4 in / 10 x 10 cm

Adjust needle size to obtain correct gauge if necessary.

COLOR PATTERNS
Work in St st in the round, following charts.

Pattern A: Follow Chart A, working 4-st repeat 30 times around. Work Rows 1-4 for pattern 5 times.

Pattern B: Follow Chart B, working 6-st repeat 20 times around. Work Rows 1-7 once.

Pattern C: Follow Chart C, working 6-st repeat 20 times around. Work Rows 1-7 once.

Pattern D: Follow Chart D, working 6-st repeat 20 times around. Work Rows 1-7 once.

Pattern A

Repeat = 4 sts

Pattern B

Repeat = 6 sts

Pattern C

Repeat = 6 sts

Pattern D

Repeat = 6 sts

= K1 in Shadow
= K1 in Olive

INSTRUCTIONS
With Shadow, CO 120 sts and join to knit in the round, being careful not to twist sts.

Place marker for beg of rnd. Work 2 rnds in St st. Alternate between solid and pattern rnds in St st as foll:

*Work 20 rnds following Chart A, then work 4 rnds in Shadow.

Work 7 rnds following Chart B, then work 4 rnds in Shadow.

Work 20 rnds following Chart A, then work 4 rnds in Shadow.

Work 7 rnds following Chart C, then work 4 rnds in Shadow.

Work 20 rnds following Chart A, then work 4 rnds in Shadow.

Work 7 rnds following Chart D, then work 4 rnds in Shadow.

Rep from * 3 more times.

Work 20 rnds following Chart A, then work 4 rnds in Shadow.

Work 7 rnds following Chart B, then work 1 rnd in Shadow.

FINISHING
Cut yarn, leaving a 40 in (100 cm) tail of Shadow for seaming ends together.

Turn piece inside out and weave in ends. Turn right side out.

Pick out the CO and graft the ends together with Kitchener stitch to form a loop.

Looking Good [EVELYN HASE]

LEVEL OF DIFFICULTY
Experienced

SIZE
12 x 75 in (30 x 190 cm) at the points

MATERIALS
Yarn: CYCA #5 (chunky/craft/rug), Schachenmayr original Aventica or equivalent (25% Wool, 65% Acrylic, 10% Polyamide; 131 yd/120 m / 50 g), Blue-Green (87), 200 g

Needles: U.S. size 10½ or 11 / 7 mm

NOTE: There is no exact U.S. size match for 7 mm needles.

Notions:
Stitch marker
Tapestry needle

GAUGE
14 sts and 27 rows in Garter Stitch = 4 x 4 in / 10 x 10 cm

Adjust needle size to obtain correct gauge if necessary.

GARTER STITCH

Knit every row.

INSTRUCTIONS

CO 72 sts and knit 1 WS row, then begin working short rows in Garter Stitch as foll:
*On RS row, stop 4 sts before the end, leaving the last 4 sts unworked; turn. Make a double-stitch and knit back across row. On each RS row, leave 4 more sts unworked at the end of the row, until all sts have been used. At beg of next RS row, CO 16 new sts and knit across, working both strands of each double-stitch tog as one st. Place marker 16 sts before end of row and turn.

Make a double-stitch and knit back across row. Work short rows again, beginning at * with the marker indicating the end of row and the sts after the marker not counted.

Work in this fashion until 7 sections have been completed, casting on an additional 16 sts at the end of each section and leaving an additional 16 sts unworked at the beg of each new section as above.

Work 6 rows of Garter Stitch over all sts, including those set aside behind the markers and working both strands of each double-stitch tog as one st.

Bind off all sts. Weave in ends.

Let's Twist Again! [ULRIKE BRÜGGEMANN]

TWISTED RIBBING

(K1-tbl, p1) across.

SHORT ROW SECTIONS

Work all short row sections in Garter Stitch using Apiretto.

INSTRUCTIONS

NOTE: The beginning of the round moves after each section.

With 2 Regia yarns held together, CO 270 sts. Join to work in the round, being careful not to twist sts. Work 2 in (5 cm) in Twisted Ribbing.

With Apiretto, work 1 rnd in Twisted Ribbing, then purl 1 rnd.
Work short rows over 30 sts as foll:
*K30, turn, make double-stitch, k29, turn, make double stitch. Continue working in Garter Stitch, turning 1 st before the double-stitch on each row and making a new double-stitch after turning, until all 30 sts have been worked as double-stitches. After the last double-stitch, work

the following 15 double-stitches as regular knits, working both strands tog.
Rep from * 8 more times.

With 2 Regia yarns held together, work 6 rnds in Twisted Ribbing over all sts (in the first rnd, work both strands of the rem double-stitches as single sts in pattern).

With Apiretto, work 1 rnd in Twisted Ribbing, then purl 1 rnd.
Work short rows as foll:
**K1, turn, make double-stitch, k1 (work both strands of double-st tog), turn, make double stitch. Continue working in Garter Stitch, turning 1 st after the double-stitch on each row and making a new double-stitch after turning, until there are 28 plain sts between the last 2 double-stitches. After the last double-stitch, work the following 15 double-stitches as regular knits, working both strands tog. After making the last double-stitch, k29 then k another 15 sts.
Rep from ** 8 more times.

With 2 Regia yarns held together, work 6 rnds in Twisted Ribbing over all sts (in the first rnd, work both strands of the rem double-stitches as single sts in pattern). After Rnd 6, work 15 more sts in pattern. Beg of rnd is back at original location.

With Apiretto, work 1 rnd in Twisted Ribbing, then purl 1 rnd.

Work short rows as foll:
***K15, turn, make double-stitch, k14, turn, make double-stitch. Continue working in Garter Stitch, turning 1 st before the double-stitch on each row and making a new double-stitch after turning, until 1 plain st rem between double-stitches. After the last double-stitch, knit the 1 single st and the 15 double-stitches (working both strands tog as 1 st).
Rep from *** 17 more times.

With 2 Regia yarns held together, work 4 rnds in Twisted Ribbing over all sts (in the first rnd, work both strands of the rem double-stitches as single sts in pattern).
With Apiretto, work 1 rnd in Twisted Ribbing, then purl 1 rnd.
Work short rows as foll:
****K2, turn, make double-stitch, k2 (work both strands of double-st tog), turn, make double-stitch. Continue working in Garter Stitch, turning 1 st after the double-stitch on each row and making a new double-stitch after turning, until there are 13 plain sts between the last 2 double-stitches. After the last double-stitch, work the following 14 sts then knit another 7 sts.
Rep from **** to the end of the rnd.

With 2 Regia yarns held together, work 2 in (5 cm) in Twisted Ribbing over all sts (in the first rnd, work both strands of the rem double-stitches as single sts in pattern). BO all sts.

LEVEL OF DIFFICULTY
Experienced

SIZE
10½ x 59 in (27 x 150 cm)

MATERIALS
Yarn: CYCA #5 (chunky/craft/rug), Schachenmayr select Apiretto or equivalent (55% Polyamide, 35% Merino, 10% Angora; 114 yd/104 m / 50 g), Sage (8172), 200 g

CYCA #1 (sock/fingering/baby), Schachenmayr Regia Angora Merino (65% Merino, 25% Poly-amide, 10% Angora; 219 yd/200 m / 50 g), Aqua (7082), 100 g

CYCA #1 (sock/fingering/baby), Schachenmayr Regia Design Line or equivalent (75% Superwash Wool, 25% Acrylic; 230 yd/ 210 m / 50 g), Frost Color (4480), 100 g

Needles: U.S. size 8 / 5 mm circular needle, approx. 32 in (80 cm) long

Notions: Tapestry needle

GAUGE
16 sts and 24 rows in Pattern Stitch = 4 x 4 in / 10 x 10 cm

Adjust needle size to obtain correct gauge if necessary.

The two Regia yarns are held together—1 strand of Aqua and 1 strand of Frost—to work the ribbing sections.

Dreamy Clouds [MANUELA SEITTER]

LEVEL OF DIFFICULTY
Intermediate

SIZE
12 x 106 in (30 x 270 cm)

MATERIALS
Yarn: CYCA #6 (bulky/roving), Schachenmayr select Alegretto or equivalent (30% Mohair, 40% Acrylic, 30% Polyamide; 34 yd/31 m / 50 g), Berry (8533), 400 g

CYCA #1 (sock/fingering/baby), Rowan Anchor Artiste Metallic (80% Viscose, 20% Metallized Polyester; 109 yd/100 m / 25 g), Rose (306), 50 g

Needles: U.S. size 17 / 12 mm

NOTE: There is no exact U.S. size match for 12 mm needles.

Notions: Tapestry needle

GAUGE
6 sts and 12 rows in Pattern Stitch = 4 x 4 in / 10 x 10 cm

Adjust needle size to obtain correct gauge if necessary.

PATTERN STITCH WITH STRIPES
Row 1 (Alegretto): *K1, sl1, yo; rep from * across.
Row 2 (Artiste): *K1 (working the paired st and yo tog), p1; rep from * across.
Row 3 (Artiste): *K1, p1; rep from * across.
Row 4 (Alegretto): *K1, sl1, yo; rep from * across.
Row 5 (Alegretto): K1, *p1, sl1 (the next st and paired yo), yo; rep from * to last st, p1.
Row 6 (Artiste): *K1, p1 (working the next st and the 2 paired yarnovers tog); rep from * to last st, p1.
Row 7 (Artiste): *K1, p1; rep from * across.
Rep Rows 1-7 once, then rep Rows 4-7 for pattern.

INSTRUCTIONS
With Alegretto, CO 24 sts and work in Pattern Stitch with Stripes until piece measures 106 in (270 cm).
BO in pattern. Weave in ends.

Poppies [STEFANIE THOMAS]

LEVEL OF DIFFICULTY
Intermediate

SIZE
13 x 63 in (35 x 160 cm)

MATERIALS
Yarn: CYCA #6 (bulky/roving), Schoeller & Stahl Semira or equivalent (80% Polyacrylic, 20% Virgin Wool; 80 yd/75 m / 100 g), Red (03), 400 g

Needles: U.S. size 19 / 15 mm

Notions: Tapestry needle

GAUGE
7 sts and 13 rows in Brioche Stitch = 4 x 4 in / 10 x 10 cm

Adjust needle size to obtain correct gauge if necessary.

BRIOCHE STITCH
Row 1 (WS): Selvage, k2, *p1, k3; rep from * 4 more times, p1, k1, selvage.

Row 2: Selvage, p1, *sl1 pw, yo, p3; rep from * 4 more times, sl1 pw, yo, p2, selvage.

Row 3: Selvage, k1, *sl1 pw, yo, k2tog (next st and paired yo), k2; rep from * 4 more times, sl1 pw, yo, k2tog (next st and paired yo), k1, selvage.

Row 4: Selvage, p1, *sl1 pw, yo, k2tog (next st and paired yo), p2; rep from * 4 more times, sl1 pw, yo, k2tog (next st and paired yo), p2, selvage.

Work Rows 1-4 once, then rep Rows 3 and 4 for pattern.

INSTRUCTIONS
CO 26 sts and work in Brioche Stitch until scarf is 63 in (160 cm) or desired length.

FINISHING
BO all sts. Weave in ends and sew CO and BO edges tog to form a loop.

Emerald [HELGA SPITZ]

LEVEL OF DIFFICULTY
Intermediate

SIZE
8½ x 45 in (22 x 115 cm)

MATERIALS
Yarn: CYCA #6 (bulky/roving), Lana Grossa Ragazza Lei or equivalent (100% Merino; 44 yd/40 m / 50 g), Emerald Green (42), 250 g

Needles: U.S. size 15 / 10 mm circular needle

Notions: Tapestry needle

GAUGE
9 sts and 10 rows in Faggotting =
4 x 4 in / 10 x 10 cm

Adjust needle size to obtain correct gauge if necessary.

FAGGOTTING
Row 1: Selvage, *yo, k2tog; rep from * to last st, work selvage st.
Rep Row 1 for pattern.

INSTRUCTIONS
CO 20 sts and work in Faggotting until piece measures 42 in (115 cm). BO all sts.

FINISHING
Sew short ends of scarf tog to form a loop. Weave in ends.

Round and Round [EVELYN HASE]

LEVEL OF DIFFICULTY
Experienced

SIZE
18 x 39 in (45 x 100 cm)

MATERIALS
Yarn: CYCA #5 (chunky/craft/rug), Schachenmayr original Extra Merino Big or equivalent (100% Virgin Wool; 87 yd/80 m / 50 g), Cloud (158), 400 g

Needles: U.S. size 8 / 6 mm

Notions:
Scrap yarn
Tapestry needle

GAUGE
14 sts and 23 rows in St st = 4 x 4 in / 10 x 10 cm

Adjust needle size to obtain correct gauge if necessary.

GARTER STITCH
Knit every row.

REVERSE STOCKINETTE STITCH (REV ST ST)
Back and forth: Purl RS rows and knit WS rows.
Circular: Purl all rnds.

STOCKINETTE STITCH (ST ST)
Back and forth: Knit RS rows and purl WS rows.
Circular: Knit all rnds.

CABLE PATTERN
Work as charted. Only RS rows are shown. On WS rows, work all sts as they appear. Work the 24 st rep 1 time across and rep Rows 1-16 for pattern.

4X2 RIBBING
*Work 4 sts in St st, 2 sts in rev St st; rep from * across.

2X2 RIBBING
(K2, p2) across.

INSTRUCTIONS
With scrap yarn, use provisional cast on and CO 45 sts.

Setup Row: Selvage, 3 sts St st, 1 st rev St st, 24 sts cable pattern, 1 st rev St st, 14 sts 4x2 ribbing, selvage.

Work in patterns as set until piece measures 43 in (110 cm) long.

Remove provisional CO and place live sts on ndl. Graft ends tog with Kitchener st.

Pick up and knit 180 sts along left edge and work in the rnd.

Knit 2 rnds.

Purl 2 rnds.

Knit 1 rnd.

Work in 2x2 ribbing for 10½ in (26 cm). BO all sts. Weave in ends.

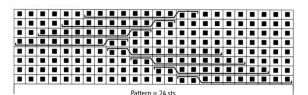

Pattern = 24 sts

■ = K1

= Sl 2 to cn and hold in back, k8, k2 from cn

= Sl 8 to cn and hold in front, k2, k8 from cn

Charts

BRAIDS & BUTTONS
Page 10

■ = Garter St (knit RS and WS rows)

■ = K1

− = P1

○ = YO

◢ = K2tog

▭▭ = Sl 2 to cn and hold in back, k2, k2 from cnn

▭▭ = Sl 3 to cn and hold in front, p1, k3 from cn

▭▭ = Sl 1 to cn and hold in back, k3, p1 fro cn

N = Make Bobble (gray): Lift the bar between the stitch just worked and the next stitch onto the left needle. Working into the lifted bar, (k1, k1-tbl) twice. Turn, purl 4, turn, knit 4. Pass the 4th, 3rd, and 2nd sts over the first. Work the next stitch, then pass the remaining stitch of the bobble over the stitch just worked.

N = Make Bobble (white): Work the next st then lift the bar between this and the following stitch onto the left needle. Working into the lifted bar, (k1, k1-tbl) twice. Turn, purl 4, turn, knit 4. Pass the 4th, 3rd, and 2nd sts over the first. Work the next stitch, then pass the remaining stitch of the bobble over the stitch just worked.

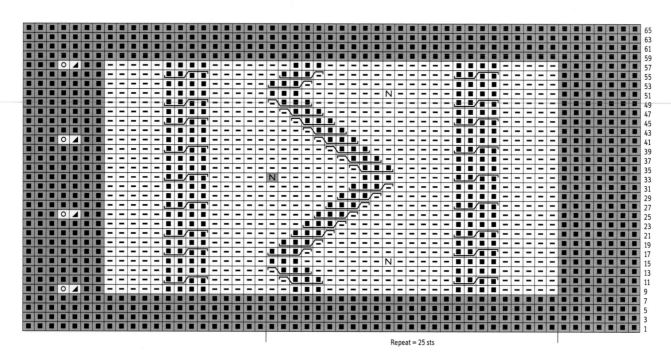

Repeat = 25 sts

BLUE TWILIGHT
Page 24

■ = K1

− = P1

▭▭ = Sl2 to cn and hold in back, k2, p2 from cn

▭▭ = Sl2 to cn and hold in front, p2, k2 from cn

▭▭ = Sl2 to cn and hold in front, k2, k2 from cn

▭▭ = Sl4 to cn and hold in back, k4, k4 from cn

▭▭ = Sl4 to cn and hold in front, k4, k4 from cn

Repeat = 52 sts

WS row

STAND OUT BEAUTY

Page 16

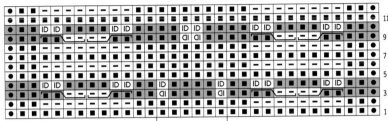

■ = K1 in Dark Gray Heather

— = P1 in Dark Gray Heather

■ = K1 in Petrol Heather

DI = Sl1 pw with Dark Gray Heather, with Petrol Heather in back

ID = Sl1 pw with Dark Gray Heather, with Petrol Heather in front

● = Selvage stitch in Dark Gray Heather

● = Selvage stitch in Petrol Heather

— ■ ■ = Sl2 to cn and hold in back, sl2 p2 with Petrol Heather in back, then k2 from cn with Petrol Heather

■ ■ — — = Sl2 to cn and hold in front, k2 with Petrol Heather, then sl1 pw from cn with Petrol Heather in back

Rep = 6 sts

COLORS ON FIRE

Page 22

■ = K1

— = P1

— ■ — ■ ■ — ■ = Sl4 to cn and hold in front, (k1, p1, k1, p1), then (k1, p1, k1, p1) from cn

Repeat = 34 sts

COOL CABLES

Page 40

Pattern Stitch

Repeat = 8 sts

● = Selvage

■ = K1

— = P1

— — — — ■ ■ ■ = Sl3 to cn and hold in front, p3, k3 from cn

■ = K1, turn and knit back

● ● = Double stitch

✕ = M1

Short Rows

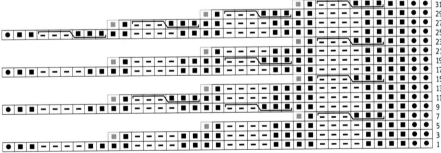

Border

VIOLET

Page 28

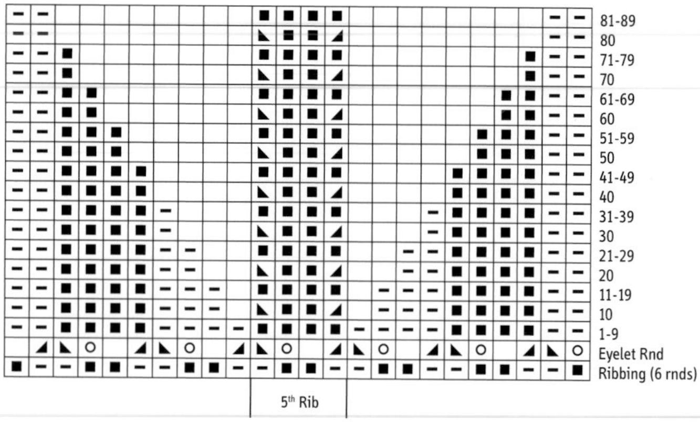
81-89
80
71-79
70
61-69
60
51-59
50
41-49
40
31-39
30
21-29
20
11-19
10
1-9
Eyelet Rnd
Ribbing (6 rnds)
5th Rib

■ = In all rnds, knit
– = In even rnds knit, in odd rnds purl
○ = Yo (on the following rnd k1f&b in yo)
☐ = No stitch
◣ = Sl1, k1, psso
◢ = K2tog

PATCHWORK IN PASTEL

Page 70

TABLE FOR COLOR COMBINATIONS

	Block 1	Block 2	Block 3
1	A + B	F + H	C + E
2	A + C	D + E	B + G
3	D + E	B + F	C + F
4	D + B	D + G	G + H
5	F + G	A + E	B + F
6	G + A	B + C	A + H
7	E + H	A + F	C + D
8	D + G	E + H	
9	B + G	E + H	
10	C + H	B + D	
11	H + H	C + G	
12	B + G	A + H	
13	C + F	D + F	

SCHEMATIC

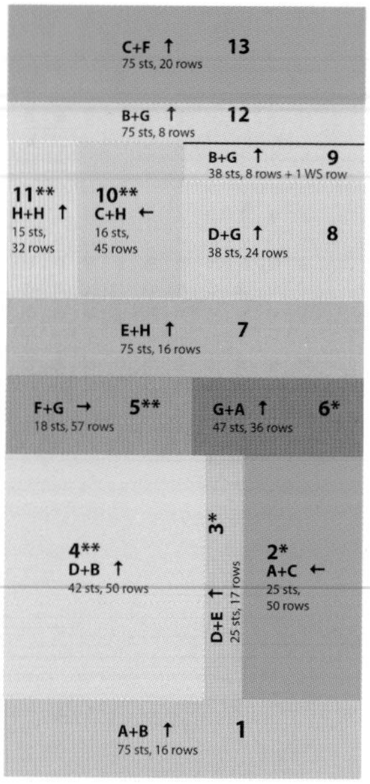
C+F ↑ 13
75 sts, 20 rows
B+G ↑ 12
75 sts, 8 rows
B+G ↑ 9
38 sts, 8 rows + 1 WS row
11** H+H ↑
15 sts, 32 rows
10** C+H ←
16 sts, 45 rows
D+G ↑ 8
38 sts, 24 rows
E+H ↑ 7
75 sts, 16 rows
F+G → 5**
18 sts, 57 rows
G+A ↑ 6*
47 sts, 36 rows
4** D+B ↑
42 sts, 50 rows
3* D+E ↑
25 sts, 17 rows
2* A+C ←
25 sts, 50 rows
A+B ↑ 1
75 sts, 16 rows

Number: sequence of knitting
Letters: colors (see materials list)
Arrow: direction of knitting
* At the end of each RS row, k2tog-tbl loop to join the last st of the new section tog with the first live st from a previously worked section
** At the end of each WS row, k2tog to join the last st of the new section tog with the first live st from a previously worked section

DELICATE ROSE PETALS

Page 30

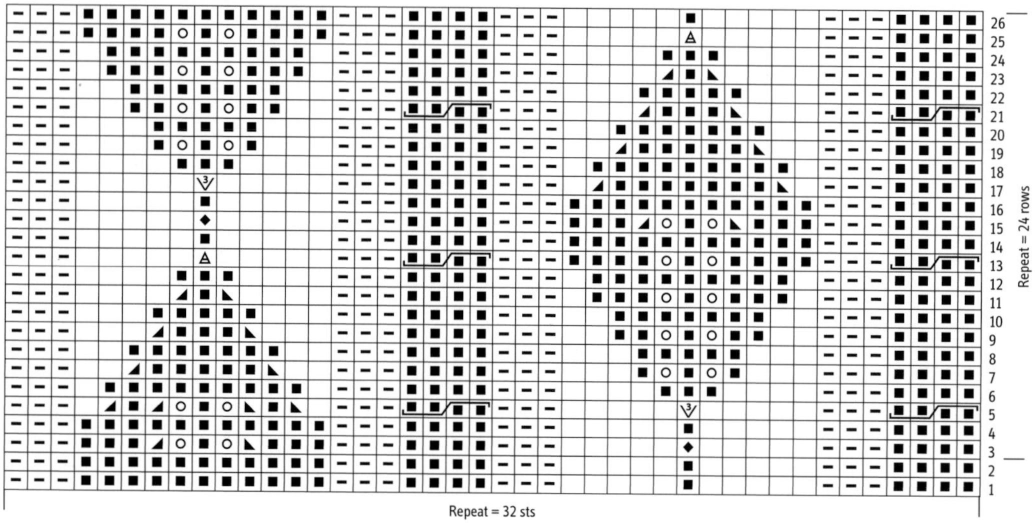
26
25
24
23
22
21
20
19
18
17
16
15
14
13
12
11
10
9
8
7
6
5
4
3
2
1
Repeat = 24 rows
Repeat = 32 sts

■ = K1
– = P1
☐ = No stitch
◆ = K1tbl
◣ = Sl1, k1, psso
○ = Yo
◢ = K2tog
[cable symbol] = Sl2 to cn and hold in back, k2, k2 from cn
[3] = (K1, yo, k1) in same st
▲ = K3tog
△ = Sl1, k2tog, psso

WATER LILY
Page 60

☐ = No stitch
− = P1
■ = K1
○ = Yo
◣ = Sl1, k1, psso
◢ = K2tog
◈ = K3tog and leave on left ndl. Then, working into same st on left ndl, (yo, k1, yo, k1, yo, k1) and drop original st from left ndl—7 sts.
◬ = K4tog
△ = Sl1 kw, k2tog, psso

FRESH FLECKS
Page 68

Spiral Pattern

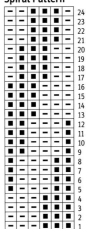

Repeat = 6 sts

■ = K1
− = P1

Row labels on right side of main chart (top to bottom): RS21, RS20, RS19, RS18, RS17, RS16, RS15, RS14, RS13, RS12, RS11 D, RS10, RS9, RS8, RS7, RS6, RS5, RS4, RS3, RS2, RS1, S14, S13, S11, S9 C, S7, S5, S3, S1, 27, 25, 23, 21, 19, 17, 15 B, 13, 11, 9, 7, 5, 3, 1, 27, 25, 23, 21, 19, 17, 15 B, 13, 11, 9, 7, 5, 3, 1, R22, R21, R20, R19, R18, R17, R16, R15, R14, R13, R12, R11 A, R10, R9, R8, R7, R6, R5, R4, R3, R2, R1

Spiral Pattern row numbers (right side, top to bottom): 24, 23, 22, 21, 20, 19, 18, 17, 16, 15, 14, 13, 12, 11, 10, 9, 8, 7, 6, 5, 4, 3, 2, 1

Repeat = 16 or 17 sts (between red and green lines)   Round begins at the red line

Charts | 93

Basic Techniques

PROVISIONAL CAST ON

With scrap yarn and a crochet hook, loosely crochet a chain with about 10 more sts than you need for your cast on. Pick up and knit a stitch in the back of a crochet chain for each cast-on stitch you need. Make sure to work in the back of the chain or you will not be able to remove the scrap yarn without cutting it later. When you remove the provisional cast-on, you will have one less live stitch than you had in the first row of knitting. To begin knitting on the newly released stitches, knit into the front and back of one stitch to increase.

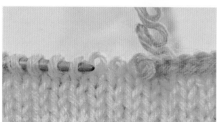

STRETCHY CAST ON

Begin just as with a regular long-tail cast on. Holding the yarn on the needle with the index finger of your right hand. In your left hand, position the tail over your thumb and the working yarn over your index finger. Hold the ends of the yarn in your palm with your other fingers to keep them tight. Lift your thumb and index finger and pull the needle in your right hand down to form a V and cross the strands of yarn around your thumb.

Insert the tip of the needle under both strands of yarn on your thumb and catch the inner strand.

Pull the inner strand on your thumb underneath the outer strand so they cross as shown below. Then pull the needle up and to the left to catch the strand on your index finger.

Pull the needle in the front under the inner thumb strand, then from back to front under the outer thumb strand. Remove your thumb from the loop and tighten to create a new stitch on the needle. Wrap the yarn around your thumb again and repeat until the desired number of stitches are on the needle.

DOUBLE STITCH

Work to the stitch indicated as the turning point then turn. The yarn is in front of the work.

Slip the first stitch purlwise. Then pull the working yarn tight over the top of the needle so both sides of the slipped stitch are on the needle and it looks like two stitches. If the yarn is not pulled tight enough, you will have a hole in your knitting later.

Bring the yarn to the front between the needles and purl back to create a short row.

KITCHENER STITCH

On the front needle, insert the tapestry needle in the first stitch as if to knit and pull the yarn through. Remove the stitch from the knitting needle.

Insert the sewing needle into the next stitch as if to purl and pull the yarn through, but do not remove the stitch from the knitting needle. Tighten the yarn.

On the back needle, insert the tapestry needle in the first stitch as if to purl, pull the yarn through and remove the stitch from the knitting needle.

Insert the sewing needle into the next stitch as if to knit but do not remove it. Tighten the yarn.

Repeat the first four steps until one stitch remains on each needle. Follow the established pattern as well as possible with these two stitches. One will be removed from its needle after the second pass of the sewing needle; there will be no second stitch on that needle to go through before moving to the other needle. The final stitch will only be entered once with the sewing needle. Fasten off.

To work Kitchener Stitch on Garter Stitch, the process is the same but the order is reversed as foll: On the front needle, insert the tapestry needle into the first st purlwise, then pull the yarn through and remove the stitch from the knitting needle. Insert the tapestry needle into the second stitch knitwise and leave the stitch on the knitting needle.

On the back needle, insert the tapestry needle into the first stitch knitwise, then pull the yarn through and remove the stitch from the knitting needle. Insert the tapestry needle into the second stitch purlwise and leave the stitch on the knitting needle.

STRETCHY BIND OFF

Knit 2 sts. Insert the left ndl into the fronts of the two sts just knit from left to right and wrap the yarn around the tip of the right needle as if to knit.

Pull the yarn through the two stitches and knit them together.

I-CORD

Using dpns, cast on 3-6 sts. Do not turn. Draw the yarn across the back of the knitting and slide the sts to the other end of the dpn. Knit the first stitch and tug on the yarn to tighten up the strand across the back of the work. Knit the rem sts. Continue to slide the sts to the other end of the needle after knitting across the row and draw the yarn across the back and tighten it after knitting the first stitch. Work cord to desired length.

Knit another stitch then work the 2 sts on the right needle together in the same fashion. Continue in this way until 2 sts rem. Cut the yarn and pull the tail through the last 2 sts.

Yarn Information

Rowan

http://knitrowan.com/store-locator

If you are unable to obtain any of the yarn used in this book, it can be replaced with a yarn of a similar weight and composition. Please note, however, the finished projects may vary slightly from those shown, depending on the yarn used. For more information on selecting or substituting yarn contact your local yarn shop or an online store, they are familiar with all types of yarns and would be happy to help you. Additionally, the online knitting community at Ravelry. com has forums where you can post questions about specific yarns. Yarns come and go so quickly these days and there are so many beautiful yarns available.